LIVERPOOL'S
GREATEST PLAYERS

THE OFFICIAL
GUIDE

YOU'LL NEVER WALK ALONE

LIVERPOOL
FOOTBALL CLUB

EST. 1892

LIVERPOOL'S
GREATEST PLAYERS
THE OFFICIAL
GUIDE

David Walmsley

HEADLINE

The right of David Walmsley to be identified as the Author of this Work has been asserted by him in accordance with the Copyright, Designs and Patents Act 1988.

First published in hardback in 1996 by HEADLINE BOOK PUBLISHING

First published in softback in 1997 by HEADLINE BOOK PUBLISHING

10 9 8 7 6 5 4 3 2 1

ISBN 0 7472 7741 9

Printed and bound in Italy by Canale & C. Spa

Edited and designed by Brown Packaging Books Limited
255-257 Liverpool Road
London N1 1LX

HEADLINE BOOK PUBLISHING
A division of Hodder Headline PLC
338 Euston Road
London NW1 3BH

PHOTO CREDITS
All pictures supplied by Colorsport

ACKNOWLEDGEMENTS
With thanks to everyone who has made this book possible; particularly to all the players who have taken time to recount their experiences and memories, the *Liverpool Echo* library for providing much source material, Graham McColl at Brown Books for editing the manuscript, to mum and dad, and especially to Lucy for all her help and support and for keeping the author fed and watered.

Brown Books would like to thank Jim Kennefick and Mike Turner at Liverpool FC for their help.

BIBLIOGRAPHY
Pead, Brian: *Liverpool, A Complete Record* (Breedon Books, 1990)
Kelly, Stephen F.: *You'll Never Walk Alone* (MacDonald Queen Anne Press, 1986)
Hodgson, Derek (ed): *The Liverpool Football Book* (Stanley Paul, 1967)
The Liverpool Football Club Official Yearbook (1980-1990)

Contents

Foreword

Football grounds are magical places. Even when empty, their grandstands are packed with the memories of every great occasion to have been played out before them; memories of epic triumphs and heroic near-misses which create an atmosphere all of their own and capture forever the roars of victory and the feverish expectations that were triggered by those famous afternoons and nights.

Nowhere are those memories stronger or more magical than at Anfield, world famous home of Liverpool FC. As the most successful club in the history of the English game, no other ground has seen the winning of as much silverware as the stadium that has been the home of the Reds since 1892. Yet the modern, postwar glories of Liverpool Football Club have not been constructed by bricks and mortar but by the great players who have worn the Liver bird motif with pride and distinction.

Any list of those players' names is going to be a long one, and from Liddell and Stubbins, through Hunt and St John and Keegan and Toshack to Dalglish and Rush it just about picks itself. Selecting one or two of the more unsung heroes and picking out the potential legends of the future, however, is an altogether more hazardous task. Consistent excellence has always been the hallmark of Anfield's finest servants, but those whose genius was – often through no fault of their own – frustratingly fleeting are also worthy of recognition, for if weight of silverware is the most lasting measure of greatness it is not necessarily the only one. Some of the contributions remembered here hopefully bear that out.

Other careers recounted on the pages that follow have only just begun and are featured not so much for what they have achieved, although in some cases that is already more than many pros accomplish in their entire playing lives, but for the potential riches that lie ahead of them. Whether those fledgling talents go on to emulate the successes of their predecessors remains to be seen, but they are undoubtedly the best bets for Liverpool's future. And as Kopites everywhere will know, Anfield rarely backs losers.

Finally, a few words of explanation regarding the statistics that accompany each player's entry are also perhaps appropriate here. All statistics are correct up to the end of the 1996-97 season. The total of substitute appearances noted in brackets has also been included in the overall total of games played, while each man's full debut is defined as the first match in which he was named in the starting line-up, ignoring any earlier introductions as a replacement. All the trophy honours listed are those won only with Liverpool and do not include prizes won with other clubs. The international caps totals listed are those gained in the player's entire career, with the exception of those recorded against the names of footballers from outside the British Isles – Bruce Grobbelaar and Jan Molby – whose tallies feature only representative appearances made while at Anfield.

David Walmsley

John Aldridge

I t took him fully 15 years, but on 27 January 1987, John Aldridge finally achieved a lifelong ambition by signing for Liverpool Football Club. Rejected by the Reds as a 14-year-old trialist, his road to Anfield took him from South Liverpool to Newport County and Oxford United before Kenny Dalglish singled him out as a ready-made replacement for the Juventus-bound Ian Rush. If the £700,000 paid for a player who was just over a year away from turning 30 caused some surprise inside many footballing circles, the manner in which 'Aldo' set about his work silenced those doubters almost immediately. He spent less than three years at Anfield, but in that time delivered a goals per game return of which even his boyhood hero, Roger Hunt, would have been proud, particularly as the former British Leyland toolmaker could not have been handed a more arduous task than the one he faced in succeeding a goalscorer who was widely seen as irreplaceable. The highest compliment that can be paid to Aldridge is simply that throughout Rush's 12-month absence, he was never missed – and not just because his successor was something of a lookalike

John Aldridge spearheaded Liverpool's challenge for the 1988-89 FA Cup, here holding off Millwall's Ian Dawes in a fourth round tie at The Den. Typically, it was Aldridge who opened the scoring with a precise header from John Barnes' cross.

in build, style and choice of facial hair. His goals tally may have benefited from his position as Liverpool's penalty-taker, but the Garston-born striker scored with such regularity from open play that he was often chosen ahead of Rush in the latter's first season back from Italy.

John began his Liverpool career much as he intended to continue, following up an appearance as a substitute at Aston Villa with a goal on his full debut, a headed Anfield winner against Southampton. That was one area in which the two strikers did differ, as Aldridge was far more prolific than his predecessor in the air. The new boy's other prime assets were a natural poacher's eye for an opening, bravery in the box and an uncanny, instinctive knack of being in the right place at the right time.

Outstanding service

To complement those attributes, he couldn't have asked for two better providers than John Barnes and Peter Beardsley, who arrived from Watford and Newcastle respectively to feed him chance after chance as the Reds set off at record pace in pursuit of the 1987-88 League title. Aldridge scored 12 times in the first 11 games of that campaign, and had bagged a total of 29 in all competitions by the season's end, but the businesslike efficiency with which he routinely found the target – as

Aldridge struck 61 goals for the Reds in the 102 games he played for the club, but few of those were more spectacular than the volley that sent Liverpool to Wembley in 1988 with a 2-1 FA Cup semi-final win over Nottingham Forest at Hillsborough.

often as not from around the six-yard box area where he was at his deadliest – meant his contribution was often overshadowed by the dazzling build up play that had gone before. Yet that is not to say that all Aldo's Liverpool goals were tap-ins, for he was never afraid to strike from further out, as he did in spectacular fashion to volley home John Barnes' cross for his second goal in the 2-1 FA Cup semi-final win over Nottingham Forest that took his team to Wembley in 1988. With the Championship already in the bag, the Double was on once more, against an unfancied Wimbledon side whom an Aldridge goal had helped see off in the league less than two months earlier. However, the biggest day of John's life ended in despair when he missed the first penalty of his Anfield career as a lethargic Liverpool went down to a shock 1-0 defeat.

The memory of that miss and the shadow cast by Rush's return from Turin in time for the start of the following season might have told on many a lesser man, but the former Kopite responded with the determination that had become his hallmark, netting twice in the Charity Shield before grabbing a hat-trick at Charlton on the opening day of the League programme. Rush was on the bench that afternoon and although he started 23 games throughout the campaign, Aldridge's was the more persistent presence in the side. So when the season reached its emotional Cup final climax against Everton at Wembley the pair were occupying the same positions as in that very first game. The Hillsborough disaster, after which the striker had considering hanging up his boots in grief, had put his penalty miss against Wimbledon into perspective, but in the 1989 final he wasted little time in making amends for it all the same, scoring after just four minutes with his first touch of the match. Rush added the other two goals in that 3-2 win, and by the time the following season kicked off it was clear that he was once again Liverpool's first choice striker. With the season less than a month old, Dalglish sold Aldridge to Real Sociedad for one million pounds.

Saluting the fans

But before he left for Spain, he was afforded one more moment of glory in front of his beloved Spion Kop, invited off the bench to convert a penalty in the 9-0 thrashing of Crystal Palace and so leave the Anfield arena in the same goalscoring manner he had entered it.

The evening ended with Aldo throwing his shirt and boots to the applauding Kop at full-time in a gesture of mutual thanks for many great memories. The crowd knew exactly how much playing for the Reds had meant to Aldridge, and it is a tribute to his contribution that they enjoyed every minute of his relatively short stay at the club just as much as he did.

Career History

Born: Liverpool, 18 September 1958
Signed: January 1987, from Oxford United
Full debut: Liverpool 1 Southampton 0,
Division One, 28 February 1987
Games: 102 (14 as sub)
Goals: 61

International Caps

67 Republic of Ireland caps, 19 goals

Honours

League Championship 1987-88;
FA Cup 1988-89

Other Clubs

Newport County, Oxford United,
Real Sociedad (Spain),
Tranmere Rovers

John Barnes

Back in the summer of 1987 there were plenty of Liverpool fans who thought that signing John Barnes was not a good idea. It took the brilliant winger about a fortnight to prove the doubters wrong as he set about establishing himself as the most devastating and flamboyant attacking force in Britain. His debut season contained a series of displays of astonishing skill, pace and power the likes of which had never been at Anfield before, and even from the periphery of the left wing he was the dominant figure of two championship triumphs achieved in the first three years of his career at the club. That form elevated him to the ranks of the few greats to be voted Footballer of the Year on two separate occasions, and he could yet win a third award after reinventing himself in the heart of the Reds' midfield on reaching his thirties. Barnes proved as pivotal an influence in that new position as he had in his days on the flank and it is not unfair to say that without the club captain's wise head among them, Liverpool's mid-1990s crop of outstanding youngsters would never have developed at the breakneck speed they did.

However, the evidence of their own eyes has never been sufficient proof of 'Digger's worth for some frequenters of the Anfield stands, and so from the very beginning he has generally enjoyed more fickle support from the fans than many of his less mercurial colleagues.

After capturing two Player of the Year awards, John Barnes had to battle back from a succession of injuries that badly affected his form during the early 1990s. He did so to such effect that Roy Evans made him team captain in season 1995-96.

Outrageous genius

True, the outrageous genius that made him an international at 19 and stunned the Brazilians with his wonder goal in the Maracana at 20 had been occasionally blunted by inconsistency at Watford. True, he didn't instantly endear himself to the Kopites when he made the Reds wait three months for his signature by holding out for a move to Italy that never materialised. True, while the nation at large has always moaned that he never really produced his club form for his country, his middle, injury-riven years at Anfield had the fans there grumbling that he was increasingly producing his England form

for Liverpool. But compared to the attacking majesty, the vision, the composure and the jaw-dropping ball skills with which he has graced the red shirt for almost a decade, those gripes merely elevate nit-picking to an

Not all Liverpool fans were convinced that John Barnes' instinctive individualism would fit into the traditional Anfield style but the powerful running, pinpoint passing and devastating dribbles that he brought to the side won the doubters over immediately.

art form. Letting his eloquent feet answer for him, Barnes has always risen above such petty criticism in the same dignified manner with which he has shrugged off the vile racism his genius has always attracted at the away grounds of the country.

A hat-trick of magic

His swiftest and most emphatic riposte, however, was reserved for the pre-debut critics of his new home turf who considered the laid-back Jamaican individualist to be out of synch with Liverpool's traditions of hard work and team play. A collapsed sewer beneath the Kop forced the Reds to open the 1987-88 campaign with three consecutive away games, at which the massive followings that travelled to Arsenal, Coventry and West Ham gave Barnes the most rapturous of receptions. He in turn responded with a hat-trick of mouth-watering displays that sparked the first of many Anfield lock-outs when the team finally returned for a match against Oxford United. And John rewarded their faith with an even more enchanting performance of bewildering trickery, weaving his magic down the left to set up a goal for John Aldridge and adding the second himself from a free-kick routine that ended with the winger curling an unstoppable 20-yarder into the net. An ecstatic Kop surrendered its heart to him on the spot.

Such celebrations became a common sight as Barnes demonstrated unerring accuracy with his left foot. A free-kick on the edge of the box became almost as good as a penalty to his team.

The Reds raced to the title that year on the back of a record-equalling run of 29 matches unbeaten from the start of the season, the majority of which were inspired by John Barnes. Moving to a team of Liverpool's power had enabled him to add consistency to his skills, as their ability to dominate opponents both home and away meant Barnes was involved on a more continual basis than he had ever been at Watford.

His new team's overall quality gave him more scope to expand his repertoire further still. Given licence to roam the inside-left channel as well as the winger's traditional touchline domain, he caused further consternation for defenders who were now uncertain as to which side he would beat them on. That he would beat them was one of the few things of which they could be sure. Blessed with perhaps the finest control Anfield has seen, he could kill a pass instantly, regardless of his position or the pace and angle at which it arrived, and could exert a similar mastery of the ball while running flat out and under the sternest of challenges.

A quick mover

Barnes' control was his most potent weapon in the confined spaces that modern wingers find themselves working in. A shimmy, a step-over, a drag-back or a nutmeg took him effortlessly past defenders completely thrown by the skill that allowed him to execute such manoeuvres without apparently breaking stride. But Barnes could also burn off his marker with the smooth acceleration that would take him into space behind full-backs in pursuit of either a through ball from midfield or his own push forward. Allied to that skill and speed was the massive upper-body strength that made him as effective in close combat as he was in the wide open spaces of the wing. Near-impossible to knock out of his stride, he could hold off several

In his twenties John Barnes was an explosive winger. Here he shoots against Everton in the 1989 FA Cup final. In his thirties, a new anchor role allowed his vision to make up for the yard of pace he had lost with age.

opponents while looking up in search of his next option. But what really captured the fans' imagination were the ball skills that illuminated every stage on which he appeared.

Although that season was a real one-off for the side that Barnes rates as the best in which he ever appeared, the player scaled similar heights as Liverpool claimed the title once more in 1989-90. After that, however, injury began to strike him on a regular basis. Although always a fearsome trainer, John had never before been faced with extended periods of inactivity and the associated problems of weight control and the long uphill pursuit of full match fitness. That these new problems coincided with the greatest period of upheaval Anfield had seen since the arrival of Bill Shankly helped neither player nor club, and the pendulum of public popularity began to swing away from him. Never the greatest of tacklers nor the most rumbustious of players, Barnes' languid style was now, in the absence of his best form, widely – and falsely – interpreted as a workshy lack of commitment.

Slowing down

However, voluntary extra work in several close seasons restored him to peak condition. Roy Evans rewarded his effort by handing him the captaincy and a central midfield role in which keen young legs around him would mask the toll that increasing age had taken on his own speed. The manager thought highly enough of his experience, vision and leadership to dub him his coach on the field. Others preferred the soubriquet of slowcoach on the field as the view spread that Liverpool needed a more dynamic and aggressive force in the centre of the pitch to reclaim the league title that remained tantalisingly out of reach in 1995-96 and 1996-97.

Barnes passed his goalscoring century for the Reds in August 1995 with an impressive brace at Spurs but the following term his match-winning displays began to become the exception rather than the rule. Evans eventually dropped his captain for the first time in the player's decade at Anfield for the visit of Paris Saint Germain in the Cup Winners' Cup semi-final second leg. Liverpool won 2-0 and although that was not enough to overturn a three goal aggregate deficit, it appeared to spell the end of John Barnes' entitlement to an automatic first team place as he remained out of the starting line-up for the final few games of the season. The pleasure that his omission gave many Liverpool supporters was a timely reminder that he remains among those players whose genius is never fully appreciated until they are no longer around to remind us of it. John Barnes may have pleased only some of the people all the time and all of the people only some of the time, but at his best he was quite simply untouchable.

Career History

Born: Kingston, Jamaica, 7 November 1963
Signed: June 1987, from Watford
Full debut: Arsenal 1 Liverpool 2, Division One, 15 August 1987
Games: 404 (three as sub)
Goals: 107

International Caps

79 England caps, 11 goals

Honours

League Championship 1987-88, 1989-90; FA Cup 1988-89; League Cup 1994-95

Other Club

Watford

Peter Beardsley

Peter Beardsley's incandescent talent never burned more brightly than it did during his time as a Liverpool player. Under different circumstances, however, his Anfield star could have remained in the ascendant for considerably longer than the four years for which it illuminated the famous old stadium. The arrival of Graeme Souness as manager saw Beardsley shipped unceremoniously across Stanley Park to Everton in order to make room for the incoming Dean Saunders, but in truth the little Geordie's days in the red shirt had appeared numbered for some time, even under the leadership of Kenny Dalglish. In his later days as gaffer, the great Scot started to alter his line-up in the light of tactical considerations dictated by the style of that week's opponents, and against the more physical sides of the then First Division that often meant leaving out the lightweight figure he had made Britain's most expensive footballer at a price of £1.9 million in the summer of 1987.

A model professional who never offered anything less than whole-hearted commitment on the pitch, Beardsley responded positively to encouragement rather than being stirred into point-proving heroics by harsh words and criticism. He took his regular omission from the side as a veiled version of the latter, and when he moved to Goodison admitted that he had done so because he felt increasingly unwanted and unappreciated by the Anfield management.

Peter Beardsley's lack of bulk often cost him his place in the Liverpool line-up when the Reds faced hostile opposition during the latter part of his Anfield career, but the little Geordie's skills shone in all company.

That was a sad note on which to take his leave, but at least he was safe in the knowledge that beyond the dressing room politics he was appreciated to the last by the Liverpool fans, who will always prefer to remember him by the manner of his entrance rather than that of his departure. For as the creative fulcrum of the three-pronged strike force Dalglish assembled on Ian Rush's transfer to Juventus, Beardsley was the architect of some of the most breathtaking attacking football ever seen on the Anfield turf. Equally at home on either foot, his shuffling, rag-doll figure belied the strength and acceleration he packed into the frame that saw him discarded as a youngster for being too small. He would perform elastic contortions to carry him, arms flapping in a puppetry balancing act, past tackle after tackle. The speed of his feet and his adhesive close-control created space for him to work his magic, although his quickness of

Beardsley prepares to cut inside a defender as he sets off on one of his trademark dancing runs through defence. Blessed with phenomenal balance, vision and control at pace, he was the trickiest of attackers for rearguards to repel.

thought and second-sighted vision made him just as effective in confined spaces. From such tight spots he threaded slanted passes through for his striking partner John Aldridge or flicked perfectly weighted balls behind full backs for John Barnes to run on to before arriving late in the box himself to ram home pull-backs at the near post. The most glee-fully received of those finishes was the one that rounded off the Reds' stirring 2-0 victory over Everton in November 1987, when Barnes' outrageous back-heel sent Steve McMahon steaming on to the goal-line from where he dragged the ball back for Beardsley to hammer it unstoppably into the Kop end goal. The other individualistic and creative sides of his game also revealed themselves countless times during his first season of 1987-88, in which Liverpool stormed to the Championship on the back of a record-equalling run of 29 league matches without defeat from the start of the cam-paign. An Anfield full house including the great Michel Platini marvelled at his jinking trickery during a 2-0 victory over Arsenal. That win was completed by Beardsley's effortless glide through the Gunners' defence. He nutmegged Michael Thomas in the process, calmly committed goalkeeper John Lukic and deftly chipped the ball over his for-lorn dive and into the net. Fittingly, it was another piece of sublime skill from the England inter-national that won the League in front of a packed Anfield that, as for almost every home game that intoxicating term, had put out the 'house full' signs the best part of three hours before kick-off. There were five games left to play when Liverpool faced Tottenham that afternoon, but Beardsley's little drift along the edge of the penalty box was followed by a curling shot into the top corner that ensured the Reds required a result in only one of them to wrap up the title.

Taking centre stage

His shooting was not always so assured, however, and so although his goals return was quite acceptable for a second striker it is as a creator rather than a finisher that he is best remem-bered. Beardsley has always been happy to drop deep into a central position to act as a link between the midfield and attack, the situation in which his dancing skills were most deadly. With Barnes flying down the left outside him, Peter had the perfect outlet at his disposal. The pair instantly formed the most dangerous attacking combination in the country to create countless chances for the prolific Aldridge. The move in which Beardsley's perfect pass was crossed by Barnes for the inrushing Aldridge to volley the Reds into the 1988 FA Cup final had been repeated many times all season, but was so well executed that opponents Nottingham Forest were powerless to prevent the inevitable.

Being a tireless worker for the team he was also a regular visitor to his own half, chasing back to rob attacking midfielders. There were, however, occasions when Beardsley struggled to get into games. The losing FA Cup final of 1988 was one such day, although none of his colleagues emerged from the match with any more credit than he, and had referee Brian Hill allowed his first-half goal to stand, instead of inexplicably awarding Liverpool a free-kick then things might have turned out differently. The following season saw the Reds go even closer to a second Double and Peter notched up the 100th league goal of his career with a stunning solo effort at Southampton. But in a campaign overshadowed by the Hillsborough disaster he did not meet with quite the same phenomenal success he had enjoyed the previous year.

Unsettling experiments

The Championship returned to Anfield at the end of the 1989-90 season and although injury ruled him out of the title run-in, Beardsley's ten goals in 29 games had already played another significant part in the triumph. However, Beardsley was given a taste of things to come that season, when Dalglish elected to accommodate a five-man defence in a tricky FA Cup tie at Millwall, leaving Peter on the bench. Similar unsettling experiments were persisted with in 1990-91. In that campaign the busy little centre-forward scored an audacious hat-trick against arch-rivals Manchester United. But he failed to string more than five consecutive appearances together until Ronnie Moran took over as caretaker boss following Dalglish's departure in the wake of the epic 4-4 FA Cup draw at Everton. That, ironically, was the game in which Beardsley scored his last ever goals in a Liverpool shirt.

The arrival of Souness and Saunders swiftly showed him the door at Anfield, but despite the disappointments of his final season Peter never bore any grudges towards his former club, even going so far as to call up a radio phone-in to defend his successor after hearing listeners criticise the Welsh international. In return, the cardinal sin of defecting to Everton was allowed to go unpunished by the Kop. That lack of ill-will, together with the revered status he still holds there, is as great a testament to Peter Beardsley's ability as any Liverpool player could ever hope for.

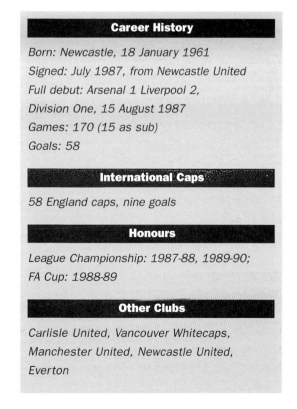

Career History

Born: Newcastle, 18 January 1961
Signed: July 1987, from Newcastle United
Full debut: Arsenal 1 Liverpool 2,
Division One, 15 August 1987
Games: 170 (15 as sub)
Goals: 58

International Caps

58 England caps, nine goals

Honours

League Championship: 1987-88, 1989-90;
FA Cup: 1988-89

Other Clubs

Carlisle United, Vancouver Whitecaps,
Manchester United, Newcastle United,
Everton

Gerry Byrne

If bravery and fortitude are as important to a footballer's make-up as skill and vision, then there have been few finer players in Liverpool's history than Gerry Byrne. Gerry, who joined the Reds straight from school, was a fine reader of the game and was always more than comfortable on the ball. But it was his iron resolve and immense physical courage that marked him out as one of the club's greatest servants, for those were the qualities that won the tough-tackling left-back an indelible place in Liverpool folklore on the famous afternoon in 1965 when the FA Cup finally came to Anfield.

During the late 1950s, the performances of club and player had persisted in much the same vein – Liverpool underachieving in the Second Division, Byrne pottering along quietly in the reserves – but with the arrival of Bill Shankly both parties' stocks began to soar. Inspired by the new boss's faith in his ability, Gerry played in every match of the Reds' 1961-62 promotion campaign and by the time Wembley beckoned three years later he had seen off all serious challengers for the left-back position. Always the strong, silent type, Byrne was by then already a firm favourite of the fans on the Kop. But his near superhuman bravery on that damp, grey May afternoon beneath the twin towers took his popularity to even greater heights. The broken neck Bert Trautmann suffered in 1956 is by far the most famous of FA Cup final injuries, while Paul Gascoigne's self-inflicted rupture of the cruciate ligament in 1991 is of course the daftest. Yet the badly broken collar bone with which Gerry Byrne played for all but three of the 120 minutes it took Liverpool to beat Leeds in 1965 is, beyond Merseyside at least, undoubtedly the most overlooked. Despite the pain of the injury, caused by a third-minute shoulder charge from Bobby Collins, Gerry played on unflinchingly to dominate the Yorkshiremen's influential inside-right, Johnny Giles, before getting forward in extra-time to collect Willie Stevenson's perfect sweeping pass and cross accurately for Roger Hunt to open the scoring. A shy, self-effacing hero, Byrne shrugged off the acclaim he rightly received for his contribution to a triumph that he always rated as more gratifying than the League Championship wins of 1963-64 and 1965-66 that sandwiched it and to which he also contributed much.

No substitute for bravery

Although lacking electric pace, Gerry always compensated for that shortcoming with fine anticipation, supreme fitness and the impeccable sense of timing with which he executed his thunderous tackles. And it was his appetite for training that Byrne believes enabled him to play through the pain barrier at Wembley, where the added stamina he had gained in the run-up to the final through putting in hours of extra preparatory work at Liverpool's Melwood training ground proved enough to carry him through. But had the same scenario been played out just 12 months later, then Gerry would not have been on the field to set up Roger Hunt's extra-time goal. The 1965 match was the last FA Cup final in which substitutes were not permitted, and so Liverpool's injured full-back had little option but to struggle on, swathed in so much half-time padding that the Duke of Edinburgh told him in the Royal Box afterwards that he looked like an American footballer.

Gerry Byrne's days at Anfield looked to be numbered when Bill Shankly arrived as manager in 1960, but the new boss wasted little time in turning him into one of the most imposing left-backs in Britain.

Ironically, while the advances of the modern game might have deprived Byrne of his finest two hours they could also have saved his career; the injury that forced the England international to quit was the same one from which today's surgical and physiotherapy techniques have helped Paul Gascoigne make a successful recovery. But in 1966 there was very little that could be done for Byrne's badly damaged knee and he was forced to look on from the touchline as what should have been his prime years passed him by.

When that 1966-67 season began, Gerry was 27 years old and had close to 300 games for Liverpool under his belt. After sharing in the England squad's World Cup triumph the previous month he was looking forward to a European Cup campaign with his club. But in the very first League game, at Leicester City, he caught his studs in the ground and twisted his knee so badly that he ruptured his cruciate ligament. Astonishingly, he returned to the first team just five months later. But despite a run of 26 consecutive matches at the start of the following season, it was clear that, even in the face of his determination to soldier on, he was fighting a losing battle. Byrne's bravery was one of the qualities that Shankly most admired in the player who, even before Wembley, had amazed him by playing more than a match and a half with a dislocated elbow. So it was no surprise that on the morning in 1969 that Gerry told his manager he could no longer carry on, the Scot accepted his decision with sadness but without question.

A hole in the heart

Shankly was quick to point out how big a hole Byrne's loss left in the heart of his team, and both the reaction of the fans and the story told by the record books confirmed that opinion. An astonishing 41,000 people braved snow, thunder and hail to pay their own tribute to the man at his Anfield testimonial match on an emotional night in April 1970, at the end of which the entire Kop stayed behind for 20 minutes after the final whistle, singing and chanting for their hero. Just three days after the historic FA Cup final win of 1965, Byrne had acted as an unwitting cheerleader for the Kop when he and fellow injury victim Gordon Milne were sent by Shankly to parade the trophy before the European Cup semi-final meeting with Inter Milan. The

pair's appearance before the heaving terrace took the already boiling atmosphere to an even higher level of intensity that sent the Italians retreating to the other end of the ground and an ultimate 3-1 defeat. Now, on Byrne's night, those same fans took the opportunity to give a fitting final farewell to such a great club servant.

A colourful character

That was one, colourful measure of the impression that Gerry Byrne made at Liverpool, and the black and white of the club's statistics tell the same story, as for fully two years after his departure Shankly's side struggled desperately to find a replacement of the same class – trying everyone from Tommy Smith and Gordon Milne to Geoff Strong and a certain Roy Evans in the number three shirt – until Alec Lindsay eventually emerged as a worthy permanent successor in 1971.

Gerry Byrne's reputation as one of the strongest and toughest players on the English scene during the 1960s was well founded. Here the England international intervenes with typical tenacity and decisiveness to break up an Everton attack during a hard-fought Merseyside derby at Anfield in 1966.

Career History

Born: Liverpool, 29 August 1938
Signed: August 1955
Full debut: Charlton Athletic 5 Liverpool 1, Division Two, 28 September 1957
Games: 330 (one as sub)
Goals: Three

International Caps

Two England caps

Honours

League Championship 1963-64, 1965-66; FA Cup 1964-65

Ian Callaghan

In a book of Liverpool records, Ian Callaghan would appear more often than any other name. His 19-year career as an Anfield professional was littered with firsts. Still the holder of Liverpool's appearances record, he was the first player to pass the milestones of 600, 700 and 800 games for the club, and his is the only name to figure in both the team that won promotion from the Second Division in 1962 and the side that lifted the European Cup for the first time a full 15 years later. He is the only Reds star never to have been booked or sent off, and he played more games in continental competition than any other wearer of the famous jersey.

Those are records that are unlikely ever to be broken, particularly in an age when signing-on bonuses and transfer-fee percentages make loyalty just about the only luxury that today's players cannot afford. It says much about Ian's character, therefore, that had his career begun a quarter of a century later he would have been unlikely to have done anything differently. The skinny kid from Toxteth who joined his boyhood heroes for a tenner was, if not quite the greatest player Liverpool has ever seen, certainly the finest servant the club has ever had. He was 15 when he signed up as an amateur and 36 when he left for Swansea City on a free transfer.

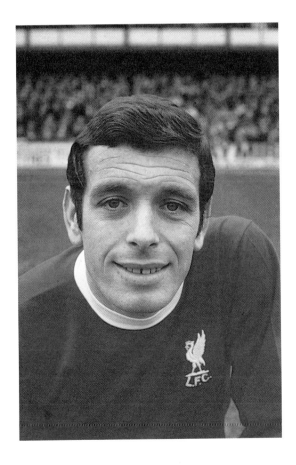

A model professional who was never booked or sent off, Ian Callaghan's Liverpool appearances record is unlikely ever to be broken. The midfielder notched up a quite incredible 848 matches in his 17 years with the club he supported as a boy.

The perfect professional

As one of the most honest, dedicated professionals of modern times, 'Cally' never took anything for granted. That attitude probably did more than anything to make his association with Anfield such a long, successful one. The other key factor behind his success was the manager who burst into the club in December 1960. Bill Shankly was immediately impressed by the fragile-looking youngster's skill and willingness, but he was flabbergasted to hear that he was spending as much of his day serving his time as a central-heating engineer as on learning his footballing trade. The blunt ultimatum he gave Ian to sign or leave had the desired effect. Freed to devote himself solely to the beautiful game it took him just a month and a half to earn his debut in the first team.

He stood in for his boyhood hero Billy Liddell against Bristol Rovers that afternoon in April 1960, and was fully deserving of the commendation that he had been the most worthy of replacements for the great man. The whole of Anfield, entranced by his precocious talent, agreed and he was applauded from the field at full-time not just by the entire crowd but by both teams and the referee as well! That afternoon, Cally exhibited the confident ball skills, eye for an opening and judicious passing that would make him such a popular successor to Liddell on the right flank. But it would be the best part of another two seasons before Shankly felt Callaghan had filled out enough to hold his own on a regular basis.

The nine appearances he made during his first two senior campaigns were followed in 1961-62 by a total of 29 outings, and it was no coincidence that Liverpool romped to the Second Division title the same year. That promotion-winning side was essentially the one that won two Championships, one FA Cup and reached the semi-final of the European Cup and the final of the Cup Winners' Cup within four years of returning to the top flight. It

Playing on the opposite flank to Peter Thompson, Callaghan formed part of the most dangerous wing pairing in domestic football. Quick and direct, he was adept at hitting pinpoint crosses while running at speed.

was packed with great players, many of whom also enjoyed lengthy careers with the Reds, but Cally was always one of its leading lights, even if, as one of the quietest members of the squad, he would never have said so himself. That modesty and faith in the ethic of teamwork shone through in his play, where he was always a provider of glory for others rather than himself, although there was no way that his all-round excellence would not attract the limelight on a regular basis.

Callaghan first made his name as a flying right winger who would hit the goal-line at pace to whip in accurate crosses for Hunt and St John. His direct running neatly complemented the swaying trickery of Peter Thompson on the opposite flank. He scored only steadily throughout his Anfield years and, although his final tally included a 1973 hat-trick against Hull City and both goals in a 2-1 win over Everton a decade earlier, he never hit more than eight goals in a season. That total was achieved once, in 1964-65, when it included the finishing touch to the cunning free-kick that

'Cally' was 34 when he picked up his fourth League Championship medal but was still going as strong as ever. Moving in from the wing during the 1970s, his performances in midfield earned him a Footballer of the Year award at the age of 32.

contributed to the 3-1 beating of Inter Milan. Cally continued his dummy run beyond the Italians' defensive wall as Hunt and Stevenson worked a move that saw the ball chipped straight into Ian's path for the cheekiest of set-piece goals.

The wing commander

That season had been crowned two days earlier by what he still treasures as his greatest moment in the game; the winning of Liverpool's first FA Cup on his very first visit to Wembley, an afternoon on which he provided the pin-point cross for Ian St John to bullet home his headed winner. And it wasn't long before Callaghan was treading the famous turf in the colours of his country, as he quickly won his first two England caps. However, Alf Ramsey's decision to dispense with wingers soon after that game cost the Liverpool star the dozens of further international honours to which his talent entitled him. Cally took that disappointment with the stoicism he showed in the face of the very roughest on-field treatment, which he would accept with nothing more than a shrug and a renewed determination to get straight back into the action. He won another two England caps – a full eight years after his first international.

By then it was Cally mark II who was starring for Liverpool. The start of a fresh decade had seen him take on a different, even more valuable role in Shankly's new Red machine. An absence caused by injury let in Brian Hall on the right, and his form was such that the manager decided he could afford to move Callaghan into the centre of midfield on his return. The little man was a revelation in the position, his deceptively spare 5 ft 7in frame bursting with the energy and stamina that allowed him to forage, run and probe with as much verve in the final minute as in the first. So consistent was he that it was only in the last two of his final seven seasons at Liverpool that Ian played less than a half century of matches (even then, he still clocked up an impressive 47 and 39 appearances), a record of reliability and service that earned him a Footballer of the Year award in 1974 and the MBE just 12 months later.

The last hurrah of Cally's Anfield career was in helping to bring home the European Cup for the first time in the club's history. Like almost all of the great Liverpool success stories of modern times, Ian Callaghan, the little boy who had pretended to be Billy Liddell while dribbling a ball around the playground of St Patrick's school Toxteth, was there at the very start of it all. His record – both as a top-class player and as a footballing gentleman – is one that deserves never to be beaten.

Career History

Born: Liverpool, 10 April 1942
Signed: March 1960
Full debut: Liverpool 4 Bristol Rovers 0, Division Two, 16 April 1960
Games: 848 (five as sub)
Goals: 69

International Caps

Four England caps

Honours

European Cup 1976-77; UEFA Cup 1972-73, 1975-76; League Championship 1963-64, 1965-66, 1972-73, 1975-76, 1976-77; FA Cup 1964-65, 1973-74

Other Clubs

Swansea City, Cork Hibernian, Crewe Alexandra

Jimmy Case

Most footballers will readily reveal that being selected to represent their country is the highest honour they can ever earn. Not Jimmy Case, however. But then, Jimmy Case was not like most footballers, and he proved that fact time and time again in a playing career that lasted an incredible 20 years and took in more than 600 league games. Around two thirds of those appearances were made away from Anfield, but it is the six years he spent at Liverpool that will always mean the most to him. Pulling on the red of his beloved team was a fantasy fulfilled for the lad from Speke who as a tiny youngster had idolised the likes of Gerry Byrne from his precarious perch on a pipe at the back of the Spion Kop.

All Jimmy Case ever wanted to do was play for Liverpool and to play well for them. And his commitment to the cause and indefatigable will to win meant he never let anyone down on each of the 261 occasions he fulfilled his boyhood ambition. Despite being voted Young European Footballer of the Year, Case never won a full international cap. He played once for England Under-23s and marked the occasion with a goal, but was never too upset at being overlooked for the full side. As the player himself puts it: 'Nothing really mattered to me other than playing for Liverpool Football Club. At that stage, I was so wrapped up with Liverpool it was untrue.' The fans' affection for Case matched his own love of the club too, for they enjoyed nothing more than seeing one of their own carry their hopes forward on the

The ferocity of Jimmy Case's shot made many a defender flinch over the years, and the Borussia Mönchengladbach players forming a wall in the 1977 European Cup final were no exception.

Anfield turf. And Jimmy was also blessed with the most crowd-pleasing attributes: inexhaustable energy and commitment, a crunching tackle, skill on the ball and one of the most ferocious – and accurate – long-range shots in the game.

Liverpool's defeat by Manchester United in the 1977 FA Cup final hurt no one more than man of the match Jimmy Case. His inspirational performance – which was capped by one of the finest goals ever to grace a Wembley final – was cancelled out by the freak goal that provided United with their 2-1 win.

Bill Shankly signed him from non-leaguers South Liverpool in 1973, for just £500, but it was not until the final day of the 1974-75 season that his apprenticeship in the reserves was completed with a graduation to the first-team. Attacking with verve and enthusiasm down the right-hand flank against Queens Park Rangers that day, he crowned an impressive home debut by winning a penalty when brought down by David Webb. If that was a fine start to his senior Anfield career, then there was better to come the following term when he established himself as a regular in the side with his invaluable mix of instinctive creativity and teak-hard toughness. The Reds took the League title and UEFA Cup that season and owed Jimmy a large debt of thanks, particularly for the latter triumph. All 11 Reds played with the midfielder's grit and resolution to emerge from a visit to sub-zero Poland with a 2-1 win over Slask Wroclaw, earned in a stadium whose dressing rooms were fitted with showers as cold as the weather. But the second leg at Anfield belonged to Case alone, as he finished the tie off with a fine hat-trick.

A dynamic performance

The former electrician scored again in the 2-1 quarter-final triumph over Dynamo Dresden that put Liverpool into the last four, but it was the 21-year-old's match-saving performance in the first-leg of the final itself that really elevated him to hero status. The Reds were trailing 2-0 to Bruges at Anfield when Jimmy entered the fray as a substitute for John Toshack and proceeded to turn the match on its head. Playing like a man possessed on the right-wing, he quickly reduced the previously composed Belgian defence to a state of panic before creating two goals that sandwiched an equaliser he scored himself, as his side ended up with a 3-2 success which proved enough to secure overall victory across the Channel a few weeks later.

Youthful successes

Case turned 24 in May 1978, and by the time that month was out he had expanded his medal collection to such an extent that after just three years of first-team football it included badges from two European Cups, two League Championships and a UEFA Cup. He had played his full part in both Champions' Cup triumphs and done more than anyone to try to complete the second leg of the 1977 attempt on the treble, scoring with a blistering half-volley from the edge of the box and turning in another buccaneering display as Liverpool's best player in the FA Cup final defeat by Manchester United. It was only in the later stages of that memorable 1976-77 campaign, however, that Jimmy had really secured his place on a permanent basis, when room in the side was found for both him and Terry McDermott.

Over the remainder of the decade he was an immovable object on the team-sheet and an irresistible force on the pitch. Despite his reputation as one of the game's true hard men, Case was a genuine ball-player who combined physical vigour with perceptive passing and vision in a similar manner to his team-mate Graeme Souness. In fact, it was only the brilliance of the tough Scot that prevented Jimmy from taking that key role in the middle of the pitch himself. Souness was still firmly ensconced in that position as the 1970s gave way to the 1980s, and a new threat emerged to Case's tenure on the right of midfield in the diminutive form of Sammy Lee. By September 1980, Jimmy found himself out of the team and although a four-minute substitute's appearance in Paris earned him a third European Cup medal, his Anfield career looked all but over.

Case was keen to fight for his place, but realised that it was a lost cause when Bob Paisley asked him if he would like to talk to John Toshack, who had inquired about taking him to Swansea. To Jimmy, that was not simple courtesy on the manager's part; it was tantamount to telling him that he was no longer wanted. So – despite turning down his former team-mate on that occasion – he left Liverpool soon after for Brighton and Hove Albion in August 1981, at the age of just 27. He left with regret but never bitterness, and his astonishing longevity over the remainder of his career – for he was never one to leave a good party early – delighted his former admirers in the Anfield stands as much as it satisfied the man himself.

Career History

Born: Liverpool, 18 May 1954
Signed: May 1973
Full debut: Liverpool 3 Queens Park Rangers 1, Division One, 26 April 1975
Games: 261 (25 as sub)
Goals: 45

Honours

European Cup 1976-77, 1977-78, 1980-81; UEFA Cup 1975-76; League Championship 1975-76, 1976-77, 1978-79, 1979-80; League Cup 1980-81

Other Clubs

Brighton and Hove Albion, Southampton, Bournemouth, Halifax Town, Wrexham

Ray Clemence

While the strikers who score the goals that win trophies are always assured of their places in the history books, no matter how fleeting their contribution, the heroic goalkeeping that so often gave them the chance to pinch their deciders is all too often overlooked. It says much about the consistent brilliance of Ray Clemence, therefore, that his name is among the first to spring to mind when footballing reminiscences turn to the Anfield glories of the 1970s.

Athletic, mobile and swift of thought and deed, the rangy goalkeeper was as dependable as he was indispensable throughout that decade of success, instilling those in front of him with the priceless confidence that stems from the knowledge that one goal should be enough to win even the toughest of matches. For Clemence could be relied upon to shut out all standards of opposition. He made difficult saves look routine and when the occasion demanded something really out of the ordinary he was rarely found wanting.

Quite apart from the sheer quality of his heroics between the posts, it was the timing of his most inspired interventions that did most to elevate him to greatness. The back four he was protected by would repel almost all invaders, but on the occasions when a period of sustained pressure finally stretched their cover to breaking point the goalkeeper would somehow manage to divert the danger. That most of those moments came when the stakes, and the pressure, were greatest does much to explain why so many of Clem's saves stuck in the memory for years after the split-second in which they were made. The man himself always singled out as favourites the stops that influenced the outcomes of matches rather than the more spectacular of his efforts, and perhaps the most vital of those was the one that did as much to turn the 1977 European Cup final Liverpool's way as the roasting Kevin Keegan gave to Berti Vogts that night. Soon after Borussia Mönchengladbach had levelled the match at 1-1, Uli Stielike broke through the centre of the Reds' defence with a clear chance to give the Germans what would probably have been a decisive lead. He did little wrong in the one-on-one with Clemence, but the superb timing of the keeper's advance and blocking dive was enough to send his shot cannoning clear of the danger area. That was just one high-profile example of the many rescues he performed in the 14 seasons he spent at Anfield before moving to Tottenham Hotspur in 1981; the others are recorded collectively in the extraordinary statistics that tell the full story of his brilliance.

A promising start

Signed from Scunthorpe United as a promising 19 year old, he understudied Tommy Lawrence for the better part of three seasons before making the goalkeeper's jersey his own in 1970-71. And although he didn't win anything that first year, an inspired FA Cup final display against Arsenal and the small matter of helping his team equal the First Division record of just 24 goals conceded served notice of what was to come. Like all the great keepers, Ray improved as he gained more experience, to peak in his late twenties, yet he had a broader base to build on than almost all his contemporaries. Tall and agile, he was always blessed with safe hands

and the sharpest of reflexes that enabled him to claw away instinctively the most unexpected or stinging of shots. Those reactions joined forces with the further advantage of reach that his long arms and legs could pro-

Never mind today's elbow- and shoulder-padded jerseys, Ray Clemence didn't even enjoy the luxury of a pair of gloves to assist his handling! But despite that basic kit, Liverpool's greatest goalkeeper had the safest pair of hands Anfield has seen.

vide to make him one of the most regular penalty-savers in the business. He could always get down into the corners of his goal very quickly for a big man, and did so twice to turn aside the spot-kicks that could have halted his team's UEFA Cup progress on both occasions that the trophy came to Anfield. The more breathtaking of those blocks kept the away leg of the 1975-76 quarter-final against Dynamo Dresden goalless, but the save he made in the 1972-73 final itself was the one that could really be said to have won Liverpool's first European prize. With Borussia Mönchengladbach heading for a 3-0 defeat at Anfield, Clem foiled Jupp Heynckes from the spot by diving full-length to his right. While the first-leg scoreline made the save look relatively unimportant at the time, its true value began to be appreciated in the return when the Reds found themselves 2-0 down inside 20 minutes and clinging on for dear life. They rode out the storm eventually, but had Ray not made his penalty save the Germans would have taken the final on the away goals rule.

An untouchable record

That 1973 UEFA Cup win came hot on the heels of Clemence's first League Championship, a competition he went on to win five times in all. The most satisfying of all the title triumphs must surely have been the victory of 1978-79, when Ray and his defence shattered their own goals-conceded record when they were beaten just 16 times in the 42 games they played – a total that is unlikely ever to be bettered and which would have looked even more untouchable had they not let in three in one match against Aston Villa.

Jaundiced observers might find it appropriate that Clem was a deckchair attendant in Skegness when Liverpool came in for him, on grounds that the defences behind which he played the majority of his football were so secure that he could have spent most games reclining on a sun lounger in the sanded goalmouth. That suggestion grossly underestimates the part played by the former Scunthorpe man in assuring his team's defensive impregnability, particularly the contribution he made when not being required to pull off save after save. Confident and authoritative when coming for crosses, he also possessed incredible powers of concentration that kept him alert enough to produce an instant reflex stop after having been uninvolved for almost the entire 90 minutes. Untroubled for long stretches he may often have been, but he was never inactive. A great talker and organiser of his defence, he ensured that those around him maintained the same state of readiness as himself, and his acute nose for approaching danger made him a fine sweeper when the need arose. If he had a weakness, it was his kicking off the ground, but that was improved by the confidence boost Bob Paisley gave him through, of all things, removing the flags from the roof of the Kemlyn Road stand once he discovered that the difficult, swirling wind their fluttering signalled had been compounding his keeper's problem by preying on his already nervous mind as he lined up goal-kicks.

A healthy rivalry

Even-tempered on the field, Ray was similarly easy-going off it and his equable demeanour meant he took what was probably the only major disappointment of his career with good grace. Although he won a total of 61 England caps, only 12 fewer than the legendary Gordon Banks, he was forced to share his country's number one spot with Peter Shilton until Bobby Robson made it clear before the 1982 World Cup that from then on it was Shilton who would be first choice.

That decision hurt Clemence but he never spoke publicly about his disappointment or held it against his rival, with whom he roomed on international trips and with whom he always remained the best of friends. Liverpool fans, however, will always believe that the final appearance scores of Shilton 125, Clemence 61 should really read the other way round.

Despite that disappointment on the international stage, however, at the club with arguably the game's richest tradition of goalkeeping excellence – even Anfield's telegraphic address is 'goalkeeper' – the name and achievements of Ray Clemence stand out above those of all others.

Career History

Born: Skegness, 5 August 1948
Signed: June 1967, from Scunthorpe United
Full debut: Liverpool 2 Swansea City 0,
League Cup, round three, 25 September 1968
Games: 656
Goals: none

International Caps

61 England caps

Honours

European Cup 1976-77, 1977-78, 1980-81; UEFA Cup 1972-73, 1975-76; League Championship 1972-73, 1975-76, 1976-77, 1978-79, 1979-80; FA Cup 1973-74; League Cup 1980-81

Other Clubs

Scunthorpe United, Tottenham Hotspur

Stan Collymore

Record transfer fees, stunning debut goals, confusion, alienation, interview outbursts, crisis talks, fines, relegation to the subs' bench, resurrection to the starting line-up and a new-found streak of creativity as potent as his spectacular eye for goal – just some of the events and emotions that Stan Collymore packed into his extraordinary first year at Anfield. Substituted in the FA Cup final and admitted to hospital just a few days later for a hernia operation that ruled him out of the European Championships, his initial season as a Red might appear to have ended on a particularly low note. But the potential he realised during the second half of the 1995-96 campaign and the promise he simultaneously showed of even better things to come, suggested that the eight and a half million pounds it took to prise him away from Nottingham Forest was money well spent.

Mixed emotions

It didn't always look that way, however, for within two months of his arrival Collymore's Liverpool career had skidded from the most sublime of beginnings to the verge of the ridiculous. He demonstrated the qualities that had made him Britain's costliest ever footballer inside 10 minutes of his substitute's debut in a pre-season friendly at Birmingham City. After beating two defenders with his remarkable power and pace, he hit a stinging shot whose rebound gave Ian Rush the simplest of finishes. He then went on to mark his league debut at Anfield by stepping calmly out of two tackles to curl sweetly home the winner from all of 20 yards. A carbon copy of that goal followed in his very next home game, against Blackburn Rovers, but just a matter of weeks later his footballing world appeared about to cave in on him. Those two strikes were the only ones he managed in his first seven starts and with his admission that Liverpool's passing and movement patterns often left him feeling little more than a spectator himself, fans raised on Rush's relentless work- and scoring-rates

Pace and direct running were assumed to be the qualities that Liverpool had paid £8.5million for when they bought Stan Collymore. He showed those skills on his pre-season debut at Birmingham City but quickly revealed he had even more to offer.

began to grumble about Stan's apparent reluctance to involve himself in team play. Then came the bombshell of a magazine interview in which he accused the club of doing nothing to help him fit into his new surroundings, and of having bought him without any clear idea of the role they would ask him to fill. A three-hour meeting with the manager, plus a private but presumably expensive penalty, cleared the air and marked the real beginning of his Anfield career.

Facing up to an image problem

Having been unfairly saddled with a reputation for being difficult and self-centred while at the City Ground, Collymore's explosion in print was not calculated to improve his image. He claimed at the time that his answers had been given off the record and blown up out of all proportion, but in retrospect they appear more of a cry for help from a man so disillusioned and disheartened that he was on the brink of giving up on his cherished chance to play for one of the finest football clubs on earth. Both parties were to blame: Stan for his unwillingness to persevere; the Liverpool coaching staff for either not recognising that the new boy was of a different breed to the majority of players who pass through their care or for failing to treat him as such. Having gone through six clubs in as many years suggests that Collymore was never one to stick things out, but also raises the thought that none of his managers ever really worked out exactly what it is that makes him tick.

He is a footballing rarity – an intelligent and deep-thinking man who sets great store by his socialist principles and his close-knit

Collymore's first season at Anfield peaked with his two-goal show in the Reds' epic 4-3 win over Newcastle United in April 1996, in which he demonstrated his talent as being among the finest of creators and finishers.

network of family and friends in his home town of Cannock. The stories that accompanied him from Forest – of Collymore being a misfit, going missing from training, fighting with team-mates and holding an unhealthy suspicion of managers and coaches – were not new. As a shy, nervous 19-year-old moving from non-league Stafford Rangers to Crystal Palace, he recoiled from the Londoners' harsh training ground banter and withdrew further and further into his shell in the face of relentless teasing about his height, his awkwardness and his Midlands accent.

Handling an individual talent

The Palace coach at the time, Alan Smith, remembers Stan as a loner who reacted to his colleagues' ribbing either by becoming riled or by thinking up a stream of excuses for not going training. However, Smith also noticed during Collymore's two years at Selhurst that he worked best in small groups and was quite happy putting in extra work in solo coaching sessions. The shaven-headed striker thrives on individual attention and seems to need the security of knowing he is wanted and valued as an integral member of the team. Nowhere has more loving care been lavished upon him than at Southend, where Barry Fry went out of his way to build up his confidence to bring out his best form. Roy Evans' brand of footballing diplomacy owes more to speaking softly than to carrying a big stick, yet he too was able to coax Collymore into only frustratingly spasmodic bursts of top class action.

Transfer rumours

The fans' patience lasted longer than that of his club colleagues, probably fuelled by a purple patch during the second half of the 1995-96 campaign in which he not only grabbed 17 goals in the season's final 29 games but also displayed a hitherto unknown capacity for creative spadework that created a hatful of goals for his strike partner Robbie Fowler. At season's end, he had added vision and creativity to the raw pace and power he had first shown. However, that run merely increased Anfield's hair-tearing frustration when Collymore reverted to his initial behaviour the following term, refusing to move north from Cannock, missing training and failing to turn up when selected for the reserves. The transfer market rumour mill swung into immediate action and inked him in for a move to his boyhood heroes Aston Villa at the earliest opportunity. With Liverpool lacking striking cover for Fowler, the Birmingham club had to wait until the end of the season for the Reds to cut their losses and unload the misfit for £7 million with a sad shrug of the shoulders and shake of the head over what might have been. Stan Collymore was not Liverpool's greatest player, but he is likely to remain Anfield's greatest enigma for many years to come.

Career History

Born: Stone, Staffordshire, 22 January 1971
Signed: August 1995, from Nottingham Forest
Full debut: Liverpool 1 Sheffield Wednesday 0, FA Premiership, 19 August 1995
Games: 81 (10 as sub)
Goals: 35

International Caps

Two England caps

Other Clubs

Wolverhampton Wanderers, Walsall, Stafford Rangers, Crystal Palace, Southend United, Nottingham Forest, Aston Villa

Kenny Dalglish

'**L**et's get out of here, before they realise what they've done.' Those were Bob Paisley's words to Liverpool chairman John Smith as the pair left the meeting with Celtic officials at which the transfer of Kenny Dalglish to Anfield had been agreed. The men from Parkhead were probably thinking the same thing, as they had just secured a £440,000 record fee for a deal between two British clubs. But over the next ten years and more it was quite obvious who had concluded the better piece of business that day. In Dalglish, who was already by far the best player in Scotland, Paisley had acquired a man who would quickly establish himself as indisputably the finest performer in Liverpool's history and, indeed, the greatest footballer the British game has ever seen.

Admirers of George Best would no doubt be the first to bristle at such a suggestion, and if we are to judge our heroes by their capacity for alcohol consumption, woman-ising and ability to go AWOL for long periods of time then it is difficult to deny the Ulsterman's claims. But Dalglish's armoury of skills was just as extensive as that of Best – if not quite as flashy – and was put to far more effective use over a far longer period of time at the very highest level. What cost Kenny the same level of tabloid adulation was his model profes-sionalism and a restrained public persona that – in sharp contrast to his warm private self – bordered on the dour and so gave the media little incentive to afford him the same superstar treatment that egged Best on towards his personal downfall. Dalglish was a footballing genius, but it is only wayward footballing genius that fills the front pages and so his extraordinary success has rarely attracted the full praise it deserves. As a quiet, family man, that suits Kenny just fine.

Authoritative praise

He has received greatest acclaim from those who really know their football: among his peers Franz Beckenbauer, for one, rates him the finest player he ever saw, while team-mate Graeme

Souness ranks only Pele and Johan Cruyff above him. And on the streets of Merseyside and Glasgow, his place in soccer folklore has been long assured.

When he arrived from his native Glasgow in the summer of 1977, already the holder of six Scottish Championship medals at the age of 26 and now driven by a desire to test himself against the sterner standards of the Football League, Kenny had the unenviable task of replacing Kevin Keegan, who had left for Hamburg after the European Cup final victory in Rome. As always, the stocky striker rose to the challenge, scoring within seven minutes of his league debut in the famous number seven shirt and striking again in each of the next two games of a first season that brought him an eventual return of 30 goals in 59 games, including the ice-cool, angled chip that won Liverpool their second consecutive European Cup, this time against Bruges at Wembley.

Dalglish's magical ball skills might not have flourished as they did had it not been for the stocky Glaswegian's deceptively powerful physique. The leg strength that surpassed anything Bob Paisley had ever seen helped him hold off even the sternest of challenges.

An impressive honours list

Those bare facts of his Anfield entrance are impressive enough, but the full roll of Dalglish honours is even more admirable. As well as winning three European Cups, six League Championships, four League Cups and one FA Cup as a player – not including the further pair of League titles and the other FA Cup he led Liverpool to as manager – he was twice Footballer of the Year, became the only man to win the classic League and Cup double as a player-boss, the only man to score 100 goals on both sides of the border, the only Scot to win more than a century of caps for his country and, with Denis Law, Scotland's record international goalscorer.

Yet that list of titles and all the goals per game figures that could be recorded tell only half the story of Kenny Dalglish's greatness. For it was the awe-inspiring manner in which he took those chances and the eye-catching excellence of his all-round game that really crowned him 'King Kenny' in the eyes of the Kop.

Touching perfection

Always a team player rather than an individual glory hunter, Dalglish was as close to being the complete footballer as one could ever reasonably hope to find. He didn't have the greyhound pace of, say, Ian Rush but as Bob Paisley once remarked, the first five yards are always run in the head and Kenny's brain was easily the fastest around. That mental agility gave him both superb anticipation and the all-round vision to recognise openings almost before they appeared. When he wasn't scoring – which was a rare enough event in itself – he was creating scoring chances for others.

While Kenny never had the height to mark him out as a centre-forward target man, his strength and powerful determination could make an aerial tussle against him into a hair-raising experience for defenders.

And when he was scoring, he was still engineering those opportunities for his team-mates, playing irresistible slide-rule passes that drew their recipients forward into the inviting spaces that his perceptive touches unlocked. Dalglish was as creative a force with his back to goal or outside the penalty area as he was deadly facing the target or inside the box.

Immensely strong legs allied to a low centre of gravity made him a supreme shielder of the ball and near impossible to muscle out of possession. Sucking defenders in, he would then fire an unexpected but immaculately weighted killer pass through the narrowest of gaps for his strike partner to finish. From the early 1980s on, the lucky man on the end of those moves was invariably Ian Rush, the majority of whose record number of goals for Liverpool were crafted by the quick-moving feet of the quick-thinking Dalglish. Indeed, anyone hearing commentary high-lights of those years for the first time might be forgiven for thinking that Kenny's surname was in fact a triple-barrelled 'Dalglish-Rush-Goal'!

The cool calculator

The emergence of Rush saw his team-mate adopt a lower profile on the scoresheet as he set about manufacturing chances from a deeper role. Even then Kenny showed he still had as keen an eye for goal as ever. His return to the side early in 1986 after a long spell out through injury inspired Liverpool to the Double. On the day the League was won it was Dalglish himself, cool and calculating as ever, who scored the decisive goal at Chelsea, controlling Jim Beglin's pass on his chest before volleying emphatically into the net.

Another goal, another grin; this one to celebrate the delicate chip that retained the European Cup at Wembley in 1978. Kenny Dalglish delighted in all his goals, but the exhibition of advertisement-board hurdling with which he followed this one suggests that the moment was more special than most.

That finish sent him wheeling away to celebrate in an image that had been repeated on television so often over the years and which is etched on the memory of every Kopite of the time – Dalglish racing towards the crowd, his arms outstretched, his face split by the broadest of beams that conveyed his love for the game and the sheer joy of scoring more eloquently than any words could ever do. Few of those scenes followed successful headed strikes, for Kenny was no John Toshack in the air. But in truth, he had no need to be, as his foresight invariably kept him one step ahead of the defence in reading where the ball would land next. On the ground, his quicksilver feet and hypnotic control made him the most elusive of opponents in the close combat of the crowded goalmouth, while there was a hard edge to his make-up that enabled him to accept unflinchingly the punishment that all skilful players in his position are forced to endure.

A lightning turn followed by a fierce, instant drive despatched with minimal backlift accounted for a fair proportion of his goals, but if Dalglish had a trademark finish then it was a rising, curling shot that would be struck either from an acute angle and whipped into the top corner of the net or from a little further out, from where it would drift deceptively beyond the goalkeeper's leap before arcing at the last moment inside the angle of post and crossbar. His 300th career goal, scored against Stoke City on 29 January 1983, was a prime example of that sly, swerving technique, but any one of dozens of equally memorable examples could be singled out to illustrate the point.

An inspirational figure

The Double of 1985-86 was the most amazing start imaginable to Kenny's managerial career with the Reds, particularly coming just 12 months after the horror and shame of Heysel, and was the start of a five-year period in which he proved himself as inspirational a figure on the bench as he had been on the field, coming within a game of further League and Cup doubles in both 1988 and 1989. That things then began to go wrong to such an extent that in 1991 he resigned in the face of mounting stress has been well documented, but should never be allowed to detract from all he achieved in the name of Liverpool Football Club. Thankfully, the welcome he received when returning to Anfield with Blackburn Rovers – to be greeted once more by familiar chants of 'Dalglish' raining down from the Kop – suggests that it never will and that King Kenny will forever be rightly exalted as the finest player ever to wear the famous red jersey.

Career History

Born: Glasgow, 4 March 1951
Signed: August 1977, from Celtic
Full debut: Liverpool 0 Manchester United 0, FA Charity Shield, Wembley, 13 August 1977
Games: 497 (16 as sub)
Goals: 168

International Caps

102 Scotland caps, 30 goals

Honours

European Cup 1977-78, 1980-81, 1983-84;
League Championship 1978-79, 1979-80, 1981-82, 1982-83, 1983-84, 1985-86;
FA Cup 1985-86;
League Cup: 1980-81, 1981-82, 1982-83, 1983-84

Other Club

Celtic

David Fairclough

In the months before Liverpool's epic 1977 European Cup clash with St Etienne, the French club's general manager, Pierre Garonnaire, flew in on a spying mission to Anfield. He left the 1-1 draw with West Bromwich Albion impressed by the likes of Phil Thompson, Ian Callaghan and Steve Heighway. But, prophetically, it was the match-saving performance of a flame-haired 20 year old by the name of David Fairclough that really etched itself on his memory. Garonnaire predicted that the youngster would soon become a regular for his country and enthused: 'I won't be surprised if, in a year or two, he is something really special. He is a good find. I always look to the future and he will be a first-team player.'

The Frenchman, who discovered international star Dominique Rocheteau, was right to sit up and take notice of the 84th-minute Fairclough goal that kept Liverpool afloat that January day. For almost exactly two months later another golden strike from the boyhood Reds fan – scored with the same time showing on the clock – crowned Anfield's most incredible night of football to dump St Etienne out of the Champions' Cup. Garonnaire was also correct in his spying trip verdict that: 'Fairclough provided the flashes.' However, he was sadly wide of the mark with his prediction that the youngster would be a Liverpool and England regular for years to come. Fairclough made only a solitary Under-21 appearance for his country and started just 88 first-team games in the nine

Playing all 90 minutes of the 1978 European Cup final triumph was an experience to really savour for 'supersub' David Fairclough, as almost half of the perennial replacement's 149 appearances in a Liverpool shirt were made as a substitute.

years he spent at Anfield. But between signing for his heroes at the age of 16 and leaving for Swiss side Lucerne in 1983, he stepped off the bench almost as many times as he was thrown into the action from the first whistle. And it was that replacement's role – together with the flashes he provided and the vital goals he scored in it – which landed him with the 'super-sub' tag he so disliked and which still clings to him so strongly that if any 'greatest ever' Liverpool side were picked to include substitutes, David Fairclough would be the first name inked in next to the number 12 shirt.

The goal of a lifetime

That reputation was born from the Fairclough strikes that turned the League Championship race Anfield's way in the spring of 1976, but it was his finish against St Etienne – the decisive final goal in a 3-1 quarter-final second-leg win that saw the Reds triumph 3-2 on aggregate – that sealed it. As if to contradict popular legend, this most famous of goals was the only occasion on which he found the net in the six times he came on as a substitute in Champions' Cup matches. But despite other personal triumphs, including a winning European Cup final appearance the following year, three League Championship medals and a 19th birthday present of the UEFA Cup, it is what he is remembered for above all else. To such an extent, in fact, that 20 years on he still reckons the goal is mentioned to him at least once every 24 hours. 'I've even

been stopped at customs in France and they've gone "Ah, Fairclough – St Etienne"!'

But even though it pains him to be remembered solely for a single moment of footballing glory, he is as proud as any Liverpudlian could be at having taken such a central role in the most dramatic win in the club's history, played out in front of a full house roaring its heroes on with chants of 'Allez les rouges!'. Fairclough, who came on to replace John Toshack, suggests that luck played a part in guiding him past three French defenders before he slipped the ball calmly beneath the advancing goalkeeper that March night, but even though his gangly style of dribbling saw him beat more than his fair share of opponents through awkward bounces and rebounds, it was his electric pace that did most to take him through the visitors' rearguard on that occasion at least.

Fairclough's directness, pace and enthusiasm rather than either raw strength or cunning posed the greater threat to opposing defences, but his overall tally of better than a goal every three games was testimony to the forward's striking effectiveness.

DAVID FAIRCLOUGH

But the good fortune he claims to have enjoyed against St Etienne was a commodity Fairclough believes he found in far shorter supply throughout the rest of his time at Anfield. Born off St Domingo Road in the shadow of the Spion Kop, Fairclough had starred for Liverpool Boys as a youngster before joining the club he adored on his 16th birthday, in 1973. Just two years later, the speedy youngster made his first-team debut – as a substitute, naturally – in the Reds' 1-0 win at Middlesbrough. His first goal for the club was not long in coming, as he hit the back of the net following his replacement of Ian Callaghan in an easy 6-0 UEFA Cup win over Real Sociedad just three days after his 1 November baptism. But it was the vital strikes he grabbed in the spring of that 1975-76 season to propel Liverpool towards their ninth League title that really made his name. There are few surer ways for a player to earn hero status on the Kop than by scoring an 88th-minute winner in the Anfield derby, and Fairclough did just that as part of a run of four vital goals in three games that proved decisive in the final reckoning.

Promising progress

The following season, he was in and out of the side and on and off the bench, while his display against St Etienne failed to earn him a place in the teams named for the finals of either the FA or European Cups. The 1977-78 campaign, however, was a happier one for the tall, awkward-looking attacker. He started 26 games, played a part in three more, scored ten goals and picked up a second Championship and a first European Cup winners' medal. He was still only 21. But over the next five years, injuries and a lack of first-team opportunities prevented him making the long-term impact his exciting early displays had promised. He felt that Bob Paisley's concern for his well-being bordered on the over-protective, and believes that an extended run in the starting line-up would have been better for his development than the predominating pattern of substitute appearances spiced with the occasional opportunity of playing the full 90 minutes. Paisley may have taken the view that Fairclough was of most use to the team coming off the bench late in a game, when his speed, directness and unpredictability were most dangerous against a tiring defence. It was a sad fact that over a full match, David often appeared inconsistent and sometimes short on stamina.

What was effectively to be Fairclough's final bow with the Reds came during the 1982-83 season when he left in the same way as he had entered the arena, as a substitute. This time he came on in the 2-1 Milk Cup final win over Manchester United and more certain finishing might have seen him sign off in style with an extra-time hat-trick. But that was not to be. Perhaps he just couldn't stand the thought of any more 'supersub' headlines.

Career History

Born: Liverpool, 5 February 1957
Signed: February 1973
Full debut: Middlesbrough 0 Liverpool 1, Division One, 1 November 1975
Games: 149 (61 as sub)
Goals: 52

Honours

European Cup 1977-78; UEFA Cup 1975-76; League Championship 1975-76, 1976-77, 1979-80; League Cup 1982-83

Other Clubs

Lucerne (Switzerland), Norwich City, Oldham Athletic, Wigan Athletic

41

Robbie Fowler

Until the autumn of 1993, there were few actions less likely to attract the attention of the men in white coats than a declaration of belief in the likelihood of Ian Rush's Liverpool goalscoring records standing unbroken for ever. In the two and a half years that followed, however, the explosion on to the Premiership scene of Robbie Fowler made the proposition entirely uncertain.

Fowler is a different type of player to Rush but his talent for finding the net from almost any position already looks as though it could be, whisper it, at least the equal of that of his mentor. To achieve even half the accomplishments of the great Welshman would be a feat in itself; an initial three-season strike rate of around three goals in every five games suggests it

is not beyond him, because – as England coach Terry Venables pointed out on handing him his full international debut at just 20 – the youngster is the most complete striker of his age the country has ever seen. Ascending to the heights hit consistently by Roger Hunt and Ian Rush is an Everest of a challenge of which Fowler is as yet only in the foothills, but as well as having time on his side he looks extraordinarily well-equipped to survive the arduous journey ahead of him.

A penalty-box predator

Two-footed, eye-catchingly effective in the air for a player of only modest height, and a genuinely instinctive finisher, there is little he needs to add to his game. He is perhaps not at his most effective when forced deep outside the penalty area, but he has the control, skill and vision that already marks him out as more than just a six-yard-box poacher, although there are few players more deadly when ghosting late into that zone than he. From further out, Fowler is a master of the unexpected, capable of the most thunderous

Robbie Fowler demonstrated his nose for goal as early as his first appearance for the Reds' senior side, recorded the Premiership's fastest ever hat-trick less than a year later and struck 86 times in his first 144 games.

of long-range drives and the most sublime moments of skill; he combined both qualities to turn, Cruyff-like, past Aston Villa's Steve Staunton and arrow home an unstoppable 30-yarder in the Reds' three-goal, eight-minute demolition of the Birmingham side in March 1996.

Possessed of the knowing swagger of a hitman expecting to score every time he steps on to a pitch, the cocky lad from Toxteth has every right to such confidence, born as it is of the unerring accuracy with which he shoots at goal. That consistency is as potent a weapon as any he owns, for almost every effort he unleashes finds the target. When eventual champions Manchester United visited Anfield in December 1995, Fowler had just four shots; only one of them went wide, two of the others hit the back of the net. The 26-yard free-kick with which he opened the scoring that day curled deliciously past the rooted Peter Schmeichel at an incredible speed of more than 70 miles per hour in an awesome demonstration of power and technique. His second showed off his composure and fine positional play as he arrived in the box at exactly the right moment to meet Steve McManaman's cross, side-step a despairing defender's lunge and dink the ball into the corner of the goal. A string of hanging headers from Stan Collymore centres emphasised his versatility, while a hat-trick against Arsenal less than a week after the Manchester United match showcased his full range of talents: scoring with a cute curler from outside the box; going through on the keeper from a Collymore flick-on; and smartly heading home for his third. Arsenal must be sick of the sight of Fowler, for he had previously kicked off his first full season by netting the Premiership's fastest ever hat-trick against them in August 1994.

A five-star performance

The top flight should have been well aware of his menace before then, however, as he had struck 18 goals in the 34 appearances he made the previous term. He scored on his debut that season, in a Coca Cola Cup tie at Fulham in September 1993, but it was the Anfield return that made the football world sit up, rub its eyes and take notice. There was nothing particularly unexpected in the fact that Liverpool won 5-0, but no one had predicted that the only name on the scoresheet would be that of the 18-year-old Fowler. He trundled back home to Toxteth in his ten-year-old Ford Escort for a celebratory Chinese takeaway that night; within little more than a year his goalscoring exploits had catapulted him into the regimented diet and luxury-car club of the first-team regulars.

The speed of his rise to fame prompted inevitable fears for his talent amid the off-field attractions that always accompany such celebrity, but with the exception of a laddish magazine interview in which he and McManaman naïvely landed themselves in hot water at Anfield, and a couple of tabloid appearances, it is only his taste for practical jokes that has caused the occasional storm in a tea cup. Trouble with his shorts at Leicester City earned him a rap on the knuckles from the FA, while an incident involving Neil Ruddock's shoes and a pair of scissors led to an altogether more painful rap on the nose from the burly defender.

When it comes to the game itself, however, Fowler is deadly serious and in his 1995-96 campaign began to demonstrate that he is acquiring the professional attitude and maturity needed to make a long-term impact at the very top. Manager Roy Evans found himself singularly nonplussed by the youngster's freewheeling approach to that year's pre-season programme and handed him the short, sharp shock of a spell on the bench when the league

Fowler has an uncanny knack of arriving unmarked inside the box at precisely the right moment to accept even a half-chance, but his gift for the unexpected makes him just as dangerous when closely watched by defenders.

began in earnest. Injury to Collymore meant he had to wait only two games to reclaim his place and he went on score 35 goals in all competitions. The bulk of those strikes – which included four against hapless Bolton Wanderers and a stunning brace against Manchester United – came in the second half of the season, when he netted 23 times in 24 games to take Liverpool to the FA Cup final and push himself into England's Euro '96 squad.

Season of glory

The following term, Fowler had to overcome early season form that was merely average by his own high standards and learn to cope with playing regularly as a lone striker, a role that did not appear to suit his style. From the statistics, however, no-one would ever have guessed that this was the case. Although his season was ended prematurely by a sending-off in the Merseyside derby when a tussle with Everton's David Unsworth escalated into fisticuffs, Fowler still finished up with 31 goals from 44 games to add to a commendation from FIFA for trying to decline a mistaken penalty at Arsenal and a fine from UEFA for displaying a T-shirt that bore a slogan supporting sacked Mersey dockers. Most impressive of all, though, he grabbed four goals against Middlesbrough to pass his Liverpool century in 165 matches – one match fewer than it took Ian Rush to reach the milestone.

As that Rush record fell and the youngster went on to score his first England goal against Mexico later in the year, the Welshman must have breathed a sigh of relief that the country of birth noted in Robbie Fowler's passport at least protects his national goalscoring total from his protégé's attentions. Good news for Rush, bad news for Bobby Charlton.

Despite his impressive first full season, Robbie Fowler was relegated to the substitutes' bench for the start of the 1995-96 campaign. He bounced back to score on his return at Tottenham in late August and added another 35 goals that term.

Career History

Born: Liverpool, 9 April 1975
Signed: April 1992
Full debut: Fulham 1 Liverpool 3,
League Cup, second round, first leg,
22 September 1993
Games: 188 (four as sub)
Goals: 117

International Caps

Six England caps, one goal

Honours

League Cup 1994-95

Gary Gillespie

J oe Fagan's decision to make Coventry defender Gary Gillespie his very first signing in July 1983 must have seemed at the time to be tantamount to fitting bumpers on a tank. Phil Thompson might just have left the club, but in Alan Hansen and Mark Lawrenson they possessed not only the safest central defensive pairing in English football, but one that looked to have the better part of a decade's continuous service still in front of it. In that light, hiring the stylish Gillespie was only topped for surprise by the player's eagerness to step into such a role. However, Gary had not come to Anfield to win medals in the Central League and, putting pen to paper three days before his 23rd birthday, was confident enough in his own ability to believe that a regular first-team place was well within his grasp. Fagan thought likewise, hence his decision to plunge into the market for Gillespie just 24 hours after taking over from Bob Paisley. He saw the signing as both maintaining Liverpool's traditionally fierce competition for places and taking care of the club's defensive future.

Off to a flying start

The new boy's precocity – he had been captain of Falkirk at the age of 17 – suggested that he would not be overawed by the Reds' stable of famous names. And while neither Hansen nor Lawrenson had ever displayed the slightest sign of complacency, Fagan elected to give Gillespie the earliest of chances to prove his worth by including him for the first game of the

pre-season programme, against Feyenoord. Sadly, Gary set a precedent of the most unwanted kind in that game, for rather than setting out an unanswerable case for starting the season, he suffered the first of the many injuries that would blight his Anfield career. And it wasn't just the nature and the regularity of the wounds, tears and strains with which Gillespie was afflicted that hampered him most, but the timing of his misfortunes. For there can be few players at any club who have suffered more ill luck on big occasions than the tall, rangy Scot. Gillespie missed out on one FA Cup final through illness and another through injury, managed to soldier through a further, losing, appearance

The total of 14 goals Gary Gillespie scored in his eight years at Anfield hides the fact that his aerial ability was equally impressive at either end of the pitch. Here, it takes a whole posse of Juventus defenders to counter his beanpole threat.

only with his head swathed in bandages, lost to a deflected goal in a League Cup final and conceded an unlikely penalty in the hollow charade of European Cup final motions that were gone through at Heysel. But in his earliest days at Anfield, getting that close to major medals seemed such an impossible dream that Gary eventually reached a point at which he felt like giving up on the chase altogether. A solitary appearance in a Milk Cup semi-final against Walsall was the sum total of his senior experience by the end of a debut season in which he watched his team-mates carry off a unique treble, and when things failed to improve significantly during the first half of the following campaign he filed a disheartened transfer request in March 1985. Fagan felt it unfair to continue depriving such an obvious talent of regular football and as he still had neither reason nor inclination to omit Hansen or Lawrenson he agreed to let Gary go, but only once the season was over, because Liverpool still needed cover on the final lap of their annual race for honours. That proved to be the best decision for both parties, as injuries to Mark Lawrenson saw Gillespie end the season with more than 20 games to his credit, including a remarkably composed 88 minutes as a substitute in Brussels.

Those matches persuaded the centre-half to reconsider his demand for a move and his subsequent decision to battle on at Anfield was ultimately rewarded by three Championship medals in his eight years at the club. The classy performances that helped win those prizes demonstrated why

The presence of Alan Hansen and Mark Lawrenson proved a major barrier to Gary Gillespie's attempts to establish himself in the Liverpool side, but when he was in the team he showed that his skill on the ball was in the same class as his two great rivals.

he had been earmarked as the ideal replacement for either of the incumbent centre-backs in 1983. Gillespie was of the same lean build as his more revered colleagues, if a little taller in height and more angular in frame, and played his football in almost exactly the same intelligent mould. While not quite as clinical as them in the tackle, he was even more dominant in the air and was the equal of all other domestic centre-halves in the constructive manner in which he brought the ball out of defence and continued his attacking runs deep into enemy territory. He appeared to have made a significant breakthrough in the run-in to the 1986 Championship, when an injury to Lawrenson allowed him to play in ten of the campaign's final 11 matches, a spell during which the side conceded just two goals and Gary scored the first hat-trick of his career, against Birmingham City at Anfield. Unfortunately, with the League won and the FA Cup final just days away, the Scottish international's jinx struck as he contracted the stomach bug that had kept Jan Molby out of the title decider at Chelsea, and he had to stand down at Wembley in favour of Mark Lawrenson.

Wembley woes

Better times were just around the corner, however, and the next two seasons saw Gillespie in the best form of his life, first forcing Lawrenson to slot in at full-back and in midfield, and then leaving him as the man trying to battle his way back into the starting line-up. His luck, on the other hand, was not about to change. Gary's first taste of Wembley ended in Littlewoods Cup final defeat by Arsenal, while after winning the league in 1987-88 he almost scuppered his chances of going for the Double in the FA Cup final when an accidental collision with Nigel Spackman in a game played after the title had already been won saw the pair spend a night in hospital with nasty head wounds. Protective headbands allowed both men to take their Wembley places but neither they nor any of their team-mates did themselves justice in losing to Wimbledon.

The next two seasons saw both Hansen and Lawrenson struggling with fitness problems that would eventually end their careers, but Gillespie was in no position to take advantage of their misfortune. He too was ruled out of the majority of those campaigns through injury. Although he did return to the side to claim his third Championship medal in 1990, his time at Anfield was obviously drawing to an end and he moved to Celtic the following summer. With better luck, he might have won the silverware and recognition his skill and resolution deserved, and which was denied him only by ill-timed injuries and the rare brilliance of the two other men who contested his position.

Career History
Born: Bonnybridge, Stirling, 5 July 1960
Signed: July 1983, from Coventry City
Full debut: Liverpool 2 Walsall 2,
Milk Cup semi-final, 7 February 1984
Games: 169 (seven as sub)
Goals: 14

International Caps
13 Scotland caps

Honours
League Championship 1985-86, 1987-88, 1989-90

Other Clubs
Falkirk, Coventry City, Celtic

Bruce Grobbelaar

It is fair to say that Anfield will never see the like of Bruce Grobbelaar again, and for those spectators with weak hearts that may well be no bad thing. With the colourful Zimbabwean goalkeeper on the field, in the next hour and a half anything really could happen; he was capable of breathtaking brilliance and jaw-dropping incompetence, the coolest of heroes one minute and the most bumbling of amateurs the next. He revelled in making the apparently impossible look routine, but possessed an almost equal talent for creating extreme danger where to uninitiated Brucie-watchers none at first appeared to exist.

And while heart-stopping acrobatics were his stock in trade, it was his excursions outside his penalty box that were most likely to induce coronaries on the Kop. Perhaps it was his natural showman's instinct and the two years of his youth he gave to the conscripts' lot of daily near-death-experience fighting in the Rhodesian War that gave him his love of risk-taking. Perhaps he just liked to be involved. Whatever, it is an unavoidable fact that the extrovert, eccentric side of his nature and the defensive clangers that went with it will always be remembered before his extraordinary goalkeeping talent.

Yet the blunders and howlers that punctuated his Liverpool career were a necessary evil; he only made them because he was attempting saves and catches that no other keeper would even dream of, and when his ambitious efforts bore fruit – which was more often than his critics would like to believe – they prevented goals that all other sides would have conceded.

Unbeatable self-confidence

Grobbelaar was blessed with the unshakeable self-belief that is so vital for those who play between the sticks, and so all criticism of his methods was water off a duck's back. It was a rare beating that took the smile off his face afterwards and his habit of berating his hapless defenders in the aftermath of goals that were quite obviously his fault was just another mechanism for preserving the confidence that allowed him to continue performing the feats that kept him in the team. His readiness to laugh at the joke that he cost Liverpool £250,000 in transfer fees and another £500,000 in lost European Cups was not appreciated in some quarters, but demonstrated his refusal to submit to the goalkeeper's fatal flaw of dwelling on his mistakes. His stock reply to the critics waiting to lambast him for his latest mistake was to judge him on what he won at the end of the season. In almost every one of his 13 years at the club, they were unable to find him guilty, for bad keepers do not win a European Cup, six League Championships, three FA Cups and three League Cups. Bruce Grobbelaar is among the finest custodians this country has seen and only his tendency to err in glorious technicolour keeps him behind Ray Clemence in the list of Liverpool goalkeeping greats.

An astounding athlete

He may not have had his predecessor's consistency and powers of concentration, but for agility, athleticism, bravery and shot-stopping prowess, Brucie – as he was always known to his fans on the Kop – was a match for anyone. A natural athlete who played representative football, rugby, cricket and baseball in Africa, Grobbelaar had lightning reflexes and a basketball player's ability to hang in the air for the split second that is the difference between a save and a goal. He never demonstrated that gravity-defying skill at a moment of greater importance than the crucial incident during the 1986 FA Cup final when Alan Hansen's blind clearance presented Graeme Sharp with the chance to give Everton the massive psychological boost of restoring their lead just four minutes after Liverpool had equalised. His header was travelling straight towards the net, which had been left unguarded by Bruce's decision to go looking for a back-pass, until the Liverpool keeper appeared from nowhere to put in a kangaroo's leap that seemed to keep him static at the apex of his flightpath just long enough to palm the dropping ball over his crossbar. The save inspired a previously rocking Reds side in which Grobbelaar and left-back Jim Beglin had almost come to blows a few minutes earlier, devastated the Blues and was as significant a turning point as the Ian Rush equaliser which had just put them back in touch. That the chaos which had reigned in the Liverpool defence moments earlier was essentially created by Grobbelaar himself was forgotten in the victory celebrations, but provided a timely reminder that while all players experience peaks and troughs of form throughout their careers, Bruce could quite merrily journey from the sublime to the ridiculous and back again all within the space of a single match.

His inconsistency brought the managers who picked him under massive pressure from public and press alike to drop him for whichever mistake was deemed to be the latest final straw. Of these storms, the fiercest came in 1983 and 1984. The first broke after his attempt in Poland at taking a difficult cross one-handed had presented an insurmountable lead to Widzew Lodz in the quarter-final of the European Cup. His next performance featured an incredible save from Bryan Robson to earn Liverpool a precious point at Old Trafford. But another gob-smacking gaffe to gift Sheffield United a 2-0 win at Anfield put the pressure right back on again. Bob Paisley, however, kept faith with the man whose goalkeeping bag contained caps with cuddly seagulls attached to the top and a selection of rubber masks for all occasions. So too did the successive managers who helped him put together a run of more than 300 consecutive appearances. They stretched from his early baptism of 1981 after Clemence left for Spurs to the start of the 1986-87 season when injury cost him the first eight games. The other manager to hold an umbrella of faith over Grobbelaar during the downpours of criticism that were regularly showered upon him was Joe Fagan, who stuck by him during a shaky start to the 1984-85 campaign which began with the own-goal that won the Charity Shield for Everton. Perhaps Fagan felt he owed his goalkeeper that much, for his outrageous antics had won Liverpool the European Cup just a couple of months earlier. The final against Roma went to a penalty shoot-out, at the start of which Joe told Bruce not to worry because there was nothing he could do in such a situation, before adding 'just try and put them off!' as the man who once scored from the spot for Crewe set off to try and thwart the Italians. And put them off he did, chewing the net for the benefit of the photographers massed behind the goal, putting off Bruno Conti with a variation on the 'Black Bottom' dance routine and forcing a miss from Francesco Graziani by wobbling around on his goal line, head lolling, as though his limbs were made of rubber. His act remained legal because he kept both feet stationary on the floor at all times, and it presented Alan Kennedy with a chance to win the trophy that he gratefully accepted.

Bruce never lost his incredible timing or the adhesiveness of his hands in shot-stopping as he reached the end of his Anfield career, and he never lost his determination to keep his place in the side. An attack of meningitis put him out of action for the better part of four months in 1988-89 and when he recovered to find Mike Hooper doing very nicely in his place he fired in an affronted transfer demand. Grobbelaar had always been a headstrong character – he once almost walked out on the club when they refused to release him for a Zimbabwe international – and this was the confidence that bordered on arrogance speaking once again. The request was turned down and Bruce responded by keeping 11 clean sheets in a run of 21 unbeaten games after his eventual recall to the side.

A peerless individual

Grobbelaar's form became more erratic in the early 1990s and the purchase of David James from Watford eventually saw him move on to Southampton. Moments like the one at the 1982 Milk Cup final when he walked the length of the Wembley pitch on his hands ensured that Grobbelaar will always be remembered with a smile. Some might say that memories of his less inspired moments still bring a chuckle to opposing fans as well, but if he is, as he always demanded he should be, to be judged on his overall record rather than simply his rapport with the crowd then throughout the 1980s Bruce Grobbelaar had few, if any, peers.

Career History

Born: Durban, 6 October 1957
Signed: March 1981, from Vancouver Whitecaps
Full debut: Wolves 1 Liverpool 0, Division One, 29 August 1981
Games: 610
Goals: none

International Caps

15 Zimbabwe caps

Honours

European Cup 1983-84; League Championship 1981-82, 1982-83, 1983-84, 1985-86, 1987-88, 1989-90; FA Cup 1985-86, 1988-89, 1991-92; League Cup 1981-82, 1982-83, 1983-84

Other Clubs

Vancouver Whitecaps, Crewe Alexandra, Southampton

Alan Hansen

If regular viewers of *Match of the Day* consider Alan Hansen to be among the hardest to please of all football pundits, they should bear in mind that he is not asking any of the players he chastises on screen to do anything of which he was not capable himself. For judging any but the very finest of centre-halves by the standards the unflappable Scot set during his 13 full seasons at Anfield is akin to expecting a team of five-year-olds to outwit Albert Einstein in a mental arithmetic exam.

Alan Hansen was the outstanding British defender of his generation, even though his style of play was as far removed from that of the stereotypical domestic stopper as could ever be imagined. A reader of the game to rival Bobby Moore, he applied a similarly cerebral approach to his work that allowed him to break up attacks without the need to dirty his hands in the process. Liverpool may have been able to call on an impressive string of

While Alan Hansen's football always looked effortlessly simple, it was his constant alertness, intelligence and speed-reading of the unfolding play that allowed him to perform in such an apparently untroubled manner.

notable hard men down the years, but their footballing creed has always been as much about anticipation and interception as it has about last-ditch bravery and freight-train tackling; and no one has ever exemplified that former approach better than the lanky 22 year old brought in from Partick Thistle in 1977.

The Scot with the lot

The £100,000 that Bob Paisley paid for what he described at the time as his latest 'insurance policy' turned out to be one of the best invested premiums of all time, as Hansen's dominance in some of the finest back fours that the European game has ever seen ensured that Liverpool's no-claims bonus was rarely in jeopardy. If one is looking to find fault with the man, then his mild aversion to aerial combat contributed to the 1990 FA Cup semi-final defeat by Crystal Palace, that left the Reds to struggle for several seasons with an apparent complex about dealing with high balls into the box. That apart, he really was well nigh flawless in technique and immaculate in his execution of his defensive duties. He may have lacked the highest gear of pace, but so good was his positional play and recovery tackling that it was impossible to tell for certain. Analyse each aspect of Hansen's game and the qualities of composure and confidence spring to mind with uncanny regularity. 'Whistling Walter' is the name former team-

mate Phil Neal uses to describe his colleague's laid-back coolness in the heat of battle, and watching him languidly stretch out a telescopic leg to deprive a charging forward of the ball before sauntering off downfield to set up a Liverpool attack, that image of carefree casualness seems as apt as any.

Despite suffering badly from homesickness during his first two seasons at Anfield and admitting to a severe loss of confidence caused by a run of bad form towards the end of the 1982-83 campaign, 'Jocky' never appeared anything less than completely at ease on the field of play, no matter how fraught the situation. However, although he may have felt at home in the First Division right from day one, it took his new colleagues a little longer to get used to his unhurried style. Ray Clemence reckoned that he needed a team of ambulancemen stationed behind his goal to cope with the

In a rare role reversal, Hansen has to fend off a sliding tackle from Everton's Graeme Sharp during the 1989 FA Cup final. The Liverpool captain was far more used to depriving attackers of a shooting chance with a perfectly timed flick of an outstretched leg.

Hansen's calm authority made him the ideal choice as skipper in 1985. Regardless of the pressure he was under, he remained unflappably cool and apparently immune to panic, always prepared to play his way out of danger.

regular heart scares he was caused by the new boy's insistence on dribbling out of defence. Thankfully, those frights soon became few and far between as the pallid, frail-looking youngster grew in maturity. An under-hit back-pass in the 1978 European Cup final caused a few flutters, but the way Hansen, who was still only 22, came through that moment to perform with increasing authority in the remainder of the match gave the first hint of the certainty he would lend to his side's defending for years to come.

Alan had made his first appearances deputising in times of injury for Emlyn Hughes and Phil Thompson, but when he established himself as the latter player's regular partner early in the 1978-79 campaign he did so with an immediate impact, as the new pairing helped Liverpool to the record of only 16 goals conceded in the 42-game league programme. At the other end of the field, although he was quite happy to extend his attacking excursions only as far as his opponents' penalty box, Jocky was a fine provider of chances.

A smooth mover

Midfield seas would regularly part in front of Hansen as he strode out of defence with the ball at his feet, always awake to the quick pass that would put Liverpool on the offensive, but while he was a regular source of shooting opportunities for others he managed to score a total of only 13 goals for the Reds himself. The finest of those, in a top-of-the-table clash with Manchester United at Anfield, rounded off a prolific run of three goals from six games during December 1979. Running on to Graeme Souness' precise pass, Hansen burst between two defenders on the edge of the box before playing a swift one-two with Ray Kennedy and finishing with some style. That ten of the centre-back's eventual baker's dozen of goals had arrived by the time he collected his second European Cup winners' medal against Real Madrid in Paris in 1981, suggests that much of his final decade at the club was devoted to perfecting his defender's art. He still sparked off many of Liverpool's better attacking movements, but in the first half of the decade his peerless displays of copybook tackling and perfectly timed interceptions made him stand out in all companies as the Reds overcame the very best that European football was able to muster against them.

As Alan's game developed to reach ever higher planes, his confidence soared along with it and even bordered on the cocky at times – witness the mid-1980s match against Manchester United in which he dribbled twice round Jesper Olsen in front of the gleeful Kop before finally ending the goading and setting off upfield with the ball. But the example that he set in his play and the manner in which his self-belief rubbed off on those around him gave Kenny Dalglish little cause for hesitation in naming him as the man to succeed Phil Neal as the Liverpool captain in October 1985. Jocky had already been one of the players' leaders off the field for a considerable length of time.

A natural leader on and off the field

Whether it was in acting as team bookmaker, organising the card schools in which he regularly bankrupted Terry McDermott or showing the way to the practical jokers in the side – he once persuaded room-mate Alan Kennedy to phone Chester Zoo, where a Mr C Lion wanted to speak to him urgently – the new skipper had always been at the front. And on the field he took the burden of captaincy almost imperceptibly in his stride, although by the time he raised the FA Cup aloft to end that epic 1985-86 campaign a combination of the pressures of his position in the build-up to that Double-winning match and the sapping heat in which it was played had left him physically and emotionally drained.

The Reds drew a blank the following term, but Hansen went on to lead the side to another Championship in 1987-88. However, by this time the knee problem that had been troubling him on and off since he had injured the joint in December 1980 was beginning to cause him more and more discomfort. An operation forced him to miss all but the last nine games of season 1988-89, although that late run still earned him a second FA Cup winners' medal, although not this time as captain, because Ronnie Whelan retained the honour at Wembley.

An eighth Championship duly arrived during the following year, but Hansen continued to be troubled by his injury and eventually he bowed out at the top, announcing his retirement in 1991. Many of the teams that he played in over 14 years and more than 600 appearances were spurred on to greatness by unfavourable comparisons with the players and sidesthat they succeeded. If they thought that they had been set a difficult task in living up to those reputations, then they should today be counting their blessings that it was not Alan Hansen's act that they had to follow.

Career History
Born: Alloa, 13 June 1955
Signed: May 1977, from Partick Thistle
Full debut: Liverpool 1 Derby County 0, Division One, 24 September 1977
Games: 607 (four as sub)
Goals: 13

International Caps
26 Scotland caps

Honours
European Cup 1977-78, 1980-81, 1984-85; League Championship 1978-79, 1979-80, 1981-82, 1982-83, 1983-84, 1985-86, 1987-88, 1989-90; FA Cup 1985-86, 1988-89; League Cup 1980-81, 1982-83, 1983-84

Other Club
Partick Thistle

Steve Heighway

Of all the whirlwind flights to fame for which football is famous, few can have been as vertiginous as the one which took Steve Heighway from university student to Anfield superstar in a matter of just a few months. And to add insult to injury for all the lesser talents whose perseverance and graft alone realised their lifelong ambition of lacing up their boots in the professional ranks, the flying winger wasn't really bothered about becoming a full-time player himself. When Liverpool signed him from Cheshire League amateurs Skelmersdale United at the age of 22, he was about to embark on a career in teaching after graduating from Warwick University with a degree in politics and economics. He later admitted agreeing to join the Reds purely because there was a better living to be earned on England's football pitches than there was in her schools. But if his motives were somewhat unusual, then the skills he displayed from the moment he first strolled into Melwood were even more out of the ordinary.

The Heighway family had left his native Dublin when young Steve was only ten, and another two years then passed before he first kicked a football to set off on his unintentional road to stardom. His natural aptitude for the game quickly took him into the England Grammar Schools' side and he progressed to play for the British Universities while at Warwick, where he stayed on to study for his teaching exams while playing for Skelmersdale at weekends. He had already turned down an offer from Manchester City while an undergraduate, but when Liverpool asked him to sign he couldn't help but give them a whole-hearted: 'Oh, alright then.'

Applied learning

He signed only a one-year contract, thinking that they would have sent him back to the chalk face long before then. As it turned out, a full 11 years passed before he left Anfield to coach in the USA and by then the Liverpool bug had bitten him so hard that when opportunity knocked for a second time in 1989, he would have swum across the Atlantic to take up his job as director of the club's youth programme.

In fact, it took only six months for the Liverpool spirit to engulf him and transform the carefree Corinthian who arrived there in

Few wingers were more dangerous with the ball at their feet than Steve Heighway in full flight. Fast and skilful, his two-footedness gave him the handy choice of beating a man either by using his pace down the outside or jinking past him by cutting inside.

Heighway gives the Borussia Mönchengladbach defence a taste of things to come during the 1973 UEFA Cup final second leg. When the sides met in the European Cup final four years later, the Irishman capped an even finer display by setting up the opening goal for Terry McDermott.

the summer of 1970 into a focused professional with the loathing of defeat that would provide a sharper edge to his easy natural ability. His educational background landed him with the 'Big Bamber' tag to go alongside fellow graduate Brian Hall's 'Little Bamber', and his student's sense of humour may not have been quite what his fellow pros were used to, but they could instantly recognise the ball skills that would serve the team so well for the rest of the decade.

Bill Shankly reckoned that his coaching staff did not need to teach Heighway anything, merely get him in physical shape, and the player himself agreed that the higher level of fitness required was the toughest obstacle he faced in making the step up from the amateur game. That's not to say he accepted his manager's opinion that he had little to learn, as he always thanked Peter Thompson for passing on more than a few essential tricks of the winger's trade during his earliest days at Anfield. It wasn't long before he got the opportunity to put theory into practice for both his club and country. An injury to Bobby Graham in September 1970 gave him his first Liverpool start, against Mansfield in a League Cup replay, just 24 hours before he made his debut for the Republic of Ireland.

Hitting the target

Shankly's shortage of strikers that season meant Steve played much of his football up front. His average of around 20 goals a season in the amateur ranks showed he knew where the target was, and he actually ended the 1974-75 season as Liverpool's top scorer with 13 strikes in all competitions. But it was on the left wing that he really made his name as the find of the 1970-71 season. Fast, direct and unorthodox, particularly during an era in which wingers were out of fashion, Heighway quickly became the scourge of right-backs up and down the land, specialising in turning defences by attacking them at every opportunity in his search for crossing possibilities from the goal-line. His centres were not always of the devastating quality of his approach work but the fact that he was able to hit them cleanly and firmly while running at top speed made them doubly difficult to defend against. Despite that skill with his left foot, the athletic winger actually favoured his right, and that two-footedness gave him another weapon in his absorbing touchline battles by handing him the option of either cutting infield or taking his man on in a straight sprint down the outside. His dribbling style was more of a fluid, swaying action than a twisting, jinking one. In beating opponents it relied more on raw speed in pursuit of balls pushed past defenders than on drag-backs and close-quarters trickery.

As a part-timer, Steve had gone past men with ease and continued in exactly the same spirit on joining the professional staff at Anfield. He told the papers that he considered football to be only a game and not so important to him in the wider scheme of things. Worldly-wise colleagues kept the cuttings and said they would bring them out in a year's time to see if he still felt the same way. He didn't of course, and the wait for that change in attitude lasted only as long as it took for the youngster's first Merseyside derby to arrive. That was at Anfield in November 1970 and the Reds' 3-2 comeback win was orchestrated by Heighway, who scored one goal himself and set up John Toshack's equaliser. The emotion that flooded the stadium after the final whistle was of a strength that Steve had never witnessed before and the feelings of elation felt by himself, his team-mates and the entire Red half of the city altered his placid approach to the game. He found himself keyed up for every match: by the 1971 FA Cup final he was the player Arsenal feared most. The Gunners completed the Double with a 2-1 extra-time win at Wembley, but they had been right to single out the threat of Heighway: he opened the scoring by skipping through the Londoners' defence to beat Bob Wilson at his near post.

Pieces of silver

His first season thus ended in bittersweet fashion, but soon the silverware was arriving in a continuous procession as Steve helped the Reds to nine trophies in the next eight years. The personal highlight of that incredible run must have been the capture of the European Cup in 1977, for Heighway capped a fine display in the final by supplying the pass that allowed Terry McDermott to open the scoring and then sending over the corner from which Tommy Smith restored Liverpool's lead.

Steve played the later years of his career in a deeper role than the one in which he had made his name. Even once he had slipped out of the first-team squad after winning his last Championship medal at the age of 31 he was still a useful man to have around, putting a move to the USA on ice to help out in an injury crisis that saw him return to the bench for the 1981 European Cup semi-final against Bayern Munich after an absence of 14 months. Although his services did not have to be called upon, it was a fitting stage on which to bow out. For someone who had not been really sure if he wanted to be a footballer in the first place, Steve Heighway had not done too badly.

Career History
Born: Dublin, 25 November 1947
Signed: May 1970, from Skelmersdale United
Full debut: Liverpool 3 Mansfield Town 2, League Cup second round replay, 22 September 1970
Games: 467 (23 as sub)
Goals: 76

International Caps
32 Republic of Ireland caps

Honours
European Cup 1976-77, 1977-78; UEFA Cup 1972-73, 1975-76; League Championship: 1972-73, 1975-76, 1976-77, 1978-79; FA Cup 1973-74

Other Club
Minnesota Kicks (USA)

Emlyn Hughes

Emlyn Hughes' record of both honours and appearances for Liverpool has few equals, and the success of his inspirational captaincy still stands almost unrivalled. But it was the heart, gusto and boisterous passion with which he played the game he loved that secured him his place in the history books as an extraordinary player in style as well as deed. Hughes was a born winner who possessed both the commitment and strength to run through brick walls in pursuit of victory, but he rarely let that single-mindedness of purpose obscure the child's joy of simply kicking a ball that illuminated his almost permanently grin-split features.

Bill Shankly had spotted those qualities, which bore a striking resemblance to his own attitude towards the game, as early as the strapping youngster's teenaged debut for Blackpool, a performance that had the Reds' boss bursting into the seaside team's dressing room straight after the final whistle to make a bid for their full-back's services. His initial approach was rebuffed but after ignoring protocol by phoning Hughes every Sunday for a progress report and to check that he was looking after himself, he finally got his man for £65,000 midway through the 1966-67 season.

A teenage prodigy

The fee was not only a club record at the time, but was then also the highest sum ever paid for a full-back in Britain, a state of affairs that might have been expected to unnerve any 19 year old arriving in the League champions' dressing room. Hughes, however, proved throughout his career that he was the last person to be overawed by any situation and was such an instant success that he went through his entire 12 years at Anfield without ever being asked to play in a reserve game.

Injury to Gerry Byrne gave him an immediate start at left-back, but by the time the 1967-68 season began he had been converted into a midfielder because as the player himself puts it: 'I had too much energy.' That verve, enthusiasm and all-action style ensured that Emlyn made an instant impact, although in his early days it was his rumbustious commitment rather than his obvious raw potential that got him noticed and that quickly earned him a nickname on the Kop.

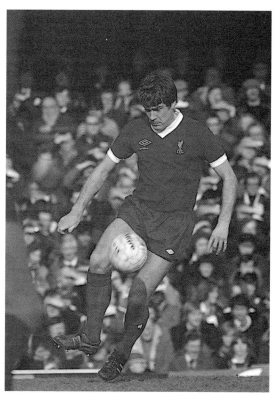

Emlyn Hughes' strapping physique made him one of the toughest defenders to play against. It also protected him from the injuries his position attracted, allowing him to miss just three games in his first nine years at Anfield.

In one of his first games, the eager youngster was enduring what would become a rare chasing, from Newcastle's Albert Bennett, and eventually settled on a flying rugby tackle as the best way of stopping his man. Fortunately, both referee and opponent saw the funny side, as did the crowd, who instantly christened him 'Crazy Horse'. The galloping colt never lost the knockabout sense of fun which prompted that unorthodox challenge. But under the guidance of Ian St John, who by that stage of his career had dropped back from centre-forward into the midfield, he soon acquired the tactical appreciation that removed the need for any repeat performances of the Bennett episode. The older, cooler St John taught his young sidekick how to put his enormous talent to best use in the middle of the park, particularly in deciding when to push forward and when to stay back, and Emlyn quickly proved himself equally adept in all situations.

Galloping to glory

When he was going forward, Hughes' huge stride devoured the ground in front of him as he steamed towards goal, using his robust strength and persistence to make considerable progress even under the heaviest of challenges. Despite being a predominantly left-sided player, he was comfortable with both feet – even playing once for England at right-back – and as he settled into the Reds midfield he began to add a new subtlety to the runs through the middle that had previously accounted for most of his attacking repertoire.

Liverpool needed all of captain Hughes' character and determination to see off the challenge of FC Bruges in the 1976 UEFA Cup final, as they came from two goals down at home and one behind away to take the trophy on a 4-3 aggregate.

Those energetic charges were still hugely effective, though, and often ended with a thunderous shot from distance that flew unerringly into the net to remind observers that he had regularly played up front as a schoolboy. One such early-1970s effort, to level the scores at Ipswich, pleased him so much that he went sprinting maniacally away to the halfway line where instant infamy awaited in the shape of a television camera that captured for posterity his succinct summary of the quality of his finish.

A similar rashness was also evident in his tackling during those early years, but experience soon smoothed out the wrinkles to such an extent that he found his greatest triumphs in the red jersey after moving to the centre of defence in 1973-74, the same season in which he succeeded Tommy Smith as club captain. Emlyn's running in midfield had always been based on power rather than pace and one of the few criticisms of his defensive play in later years was that he was slow to cover the ground, yet he more than made up for that shortcoming with his

exceptional positional play and was always worthy of his reputation as one of the finest retrievers of breakaway attacks. His tackling was still as meaty as ever and each chal-

Hughes' final campaign as skipper ended with him becoming the first Englishman to hold aloft the European Cup in successive seasons, as he led Liverpool to a 1-0 win over FC Bruges at Wembley in 1978.

lenge was met with the full force of his solid frame. Hughes' father had been a Welsh Rugby League international so it was perhaps not unexpected that his son had inherited a physique that would not have been out of place in the more physical oval ball code and whose strength was kept up by its owner's prodigious appetite – although his thoroughness at the dining table was not quite matched by a similar skill in front of the stove. Alun Evans, with whom he shared digs at the start of the 1970s, used to reckon that he never needed a diary to remind him that it was Wednesday – the night on which Emlyn had to cook his own dinner – as the smell of burning coming from the kitchen did the job just as effectively.

On the field, the England captain's footballing tastes altered with the broader experience his changes of position brought, and it was on the occasions when he operated as a sweeper when he gained the most pleasure. His initial move into defence also created a fine partner-ship with Phil Thompson, one in which Hughes now took on the role of senior pro, cajoling and castigating the tyro alongside him through the helter-skelter of his first full season of league football. The newcomer's ability in the air allowed his experienced colleague to concentrate on earthbound duties and the pairing flourished as Liverpool headed for the 1974 FA Cup final.

Since hanging up his boots, Emlyn's regular outspokenness has not always endeared him to everyone in football – and indeed even those inside Anfield – but in the run-up to Wembley he was happy to leave all the shouting to Newcastle striker Malcolm Macdonald, claiming instead that 'my game could be improved 100 per cent. My speed's bad, my control's poor and I should be able to see things coming far better than I do.' He went on to say of his famed strength: 'I'm pathetic; I couldn't lift a bag of sweets.' More than a little bit of kidology might have been suspected there, and the case was proven in what turned out to be one of the most one-sided finals of modern times as Liverpool strolled to a 3-0 win in which Hughes and Thompson allowed the boastful Macdonald scarcely a single kick.

The captain's winning ways

So the season ended with the first of what would be a seemingly endless series of images of Emlyn's beaming face beneath one of Europe's most prestigious pieces of silverware. That term it was the FA Cup, two years later it was first the League Championship and then the UEFA Cup, 12 months after that it was another Championship and the European Cup, and his final campaign as leader ended with him holding aloft the Champions' Cup once more. His massive contribution to all those triumphs, and several that had gone before, was recognised in 1977 when he won the football writers' Player of the Year award, while to really confirm his quality there was also the small matter of his status as the winner of more caps as a Liverpool player than any other of the club's servants.

The mere three matches that Hughes missed during the first nine years of his 657-game Anfield career also stand testimony to his reliability and resilience, but the wear and tear that he accumulated along the way ended his time with the Reds by causing early arthritis in his right knee. His love of the game earned him another five years playing at the lower levels following his departure from Merseyside in 1979, and he gave his final clubs the same enthusiasm that had made him such a hero of the Kop. Whatever the match, Emlyn Hughes led by example. His was a standard that inspired the men around him to the greatest of Liverpool's glories.

Career History

Born: Barrow, 28 August 1947
Signed: February 1967, from Blackpool
Full debut: Liverpool 2 Stoke City 1, Division One, 4 March 1967
Games: 657
Goals: 48

International Caps

62 England caps, one goal

Honours

European Cup 1976-77, 1977-78; UEFA Cup 1972-73, 1975-76; League Championship 1972-73, 1975-76, 1976-77, 1978-79; FA Cup 1973-74

Other Clubs

Blackpool, Wolverhampton Wanderers, Rotherham United, Hull City, Mansfield Town, Swansea City

Roger Hunt

Of all the great players to parade their skills on the Anfield turf, only one of them was ever knighted by the Kop. The recipient of that honour was of course 'Sir' Roger Hunt, as the fans on the famous terrace christened him to recognise his outstanding goal-scoring contribution to the Liverpool cause. Shankly's all-conquering side of the 1960s was packed with class, but without the decisive finishing of the quiet lad from Lancashire they might never have attained the dizzy heights they scaled during that decade of success.

Roger's goalscoring record was phenomenal and stands comparison with the best that any other striker has offered. Ian Rush may have passed his overall total for the Reds – a feat many thought would never be achieved – but no one has scored more League goals for the club or reached the 50 mark in fewer games than Hunt. Furthermore, he hit his 285 Liverpool goals in just over 200 more matches, struck a record 41 times in 41 games during the promotion campaign of 1961-62, returned hauls of 31 and 30 League goals in the Championship seasons of 1963-64 and 1965-66, and was top scorer in nine of his ten full seasons at the club. Hunt was never the most ostentatiously skilful of forwards, although his ball control and sureness of touch were always more than adequate. He preferred to go quietly and effectively about his business of hitting the back of the net.

An unselfish worker for the team

His favoured tools of the trade were blistering pace, kick-started by a jolting burst of acceleration, the physical strength that bought him extra time and space in the congested penalty box, a rocket of a shot and the seemingly inexhaustible stamina which fuelled his selfless working and chasing when not in possession. Signing for Liverpool on completion of his national service in the summer of 1959, the then 21 year old made the most immediate of impacts. Phil Taylor, soon to be succeeded by Bill Shankly, handed Roger a home league debut against Scunthorpe United before September was even a fortnight old, and he repaid that faith in 64 minutes by rattling Jimmy Melia's short free-kick in off the underside of the bar with an emphatic finish that would soon become a familiar feature of Saturday afternoons at Anfield. A total of 21 goals in 36 games that season confirmed his promise, but it was with the arrival of a new striking partner in the shape of Ian St John at the beginning of the 1961-62 campaign that Hunt's form really began to catch

Roger Hunt was the first in a long line of great Liverpool strikers, and his record of 285 goals scored at a rate of more than one every two games still stands comparison with the tallies of football's most famous names.

fire. The pair were noticeably different characters – Hunt the cool-tempered leader of
the line with a born marksman's unwavering
eye for goal, St John the fiery little terrier

*Hunt fires in a shot on the Leeds United goal during the
1965 FA Cup final. 'Sir' Roger opened the scoring in
Liverpool's 2-1 win that day and 12 months later became
a World Cup winner on the same pitch.*

whose vision made him as fine a creator as a finisher – but they complemented each other
beautifully, first in tandem up front and then later when St John was dropped deeper to dissect
defences from midfield. Roger too had more sides to his game than the one he displayed so
devastatingly in front of goal, possessing the tactical nous to create space for himself and
others through intelligent running off the ball and the perseverance to keep plugging away when
he did hit the occasional barren patch. Those spells without scoring were few and far between,
however, and at his peak in the mid-1960s he had few equals in the English game. Hunt's
most memorable season came exactly halfway through that decade, because the FA Cup year
of 1964-65 was probably of greater historical significance to the club than the twin
Championship triumphs that flanked it, as the game's most famous knockout trophy had never
resided at Anfield in the 72 years of Liverpool's existence.

A pair of Hunt goals saved the Reds' blushes against the Football League's bottom side,
Stockport County, in the fourth round and another against bogey team Leicester City was
enough to set up a semi-final clash with Chelsea. Hunt was not needed on the scoresheet that
afternoon and instead saved his most important effort for the Wembley final against Leeds
United. Goalless at full-time, his stooping header from Gerry Byrne's cross put Liverpool on
course for an historic and long-awaited victory. Roger rates that final goal and the one against
Leicester – volleyed past Gordon Banks after Ron Yeats had headed down Chris Lawler's cross
– as among his favourite strikes in the red jersey, as much for their importance as for their

quality. Coincidentally, another of his best-loved goals also came in that same season, for the march towards Wembley was matched stride for stride by progress in the European Cup. The semi-final first-leg, played just two days after the FA Cup triumph, went down as one of the greatest nights in Anfield history as Liverpool laid waste the defence of Inter Milan, at that time European Cup holders and club champions of the world, by a margin of three goals to one. Hunt's instincts and finely timed runs earned him many so-called simple finishes, but the strike with which he beat the most feared defence in football after just four minutes' play was one of his most spectacular efforts, a searing volley from Ian Callaghan's cross.

International incidents

The 1965-66 season should have been even more memorable. Although victory in the League was followed by defeat in the European Cup-Winners' Cup final, Roger still had a World Cup to look forward to with England. But although he enjoyed playing his full part in helping lift the Jules Rimet trophy that summer, the tournament marked the beginning of what became a sad, unfitting end to his international career. Despite scoring vital goals in the early rounds, Roger remains the least honoured of that England side and afterwards became the victim of a torrent of unfair criticism that bordered on a vendetta simply because he had been perceived as the man who deprived the then national hero Jimmy Greaves of a place in the side. Ironically, Hunt and Greaves had begun the tournament playing alongside each other and so it was actually Geoff Hurst who replaced the Londoner when injury forced him to drop out. Alf Ramsey kept faith with the new pairing for the final against West Germany, and while Hunt's unselfish work-aholic performance delighted his manager it did not find favour with the wider public who had demanded the return of Greaves. Eventually, Roger felt able to end his persecution only by making himself unavailable for selection a couple of years later.

A local hero

Fortunately, Merseyside has never cared very much about what the rest of the country thinks and at his beloved Anfield Hunt was always guaranteed a hero's welcome. So much so that after he had moved to Bolton in 1969 at the age of 31 a 56,000 full house turned out for his testimonial game in 1972. The service that Roger Hunt gave the club made him a worthy recipient of that tribute, and the salute that the Anfield crowd afforded him that night was not merely a recognition of the volume of goals that he recorded in their colours, but also of the proportion of those strikes that were scored when the pressure was greatest and the stakes were highest.

Career History

Born: Golborne, Lancashire, 20 July 1938
Signed: May 1959
Full debut: Liverpool 2 Scunthorpe United 0, Division Two, 9 September 1959
Games: 489 (five as sub)
Goals: 285

International Caps

34 England caps, 18 goals

Honours

League Championship 1963-64, 1965-66; FA Cup 1964-65

Other Club

Bolton Wanderers

David James

Once upon a time, keeping goal behind a Liverpool defence was seen as being among the quietest forms of part-time employment. If David James was a subscriber to that view when he arrived at Anfield for one million pounds in the summer of 1992 then a ruder awakening than the one that awaited him is impossible to imagine. Handed an opening-day debut behind an increasingly madcap rearguard, he found himself powerless to prevent a 1-0 defeat that triggered a downward spiral in which 20 goals flashed past him in 11 matches, before Graeme Souness withdrew his shell-shocked keeper from the firing line. The tactical retreat was ordered in the aftermath of a farcical 4-4 cup draw with lowly Chesterfield and the manager was at pains to make it clear that the move had been made merely to protect the 22 year old from his own defenders, rather than to register any sort of vote of no-confidence in his ability. That point was quickly emphasised by the returning Bruce Grobbelaar's concession of a further 12 goals in his first seven matches and it wasn't long before Mike Hooper took his turn in the Aunt Sally stall.

David James endured a confidence-sapping start to his Liverpool career before a run of more than 100 consecutive appearances saw him mature into one of the country's finest keepers by the end of the 1995-96 season.

England's best man

Although James returned to the team in the closing months of the season, his earlier experiences continued to haunt him. It took another 12 months for him to fully recover from them. He played only 13 times for the first-team during that period and later confessed that the whole situation left his confidence shot to pieces and threw him into the depths of depression. For a footballer whose game is built on self-belief, that was a major problem which could have finished the top-flight career of many a lesser man. That James showed the resilience to work his way back from the brink to establish himself as the finest young keeper in England is as impressive in itself as the timescale in which that transformation was achieved.

The turning point for the former Watford man came not with the departure of Souness in January 1994, but with the free transfer of Grobbelaar in the summer of the same year. The great goalkeeper had become something of a spectre to his young

apprentice, who felt overshadowed by his mere presence around the club. James felt that he had to live up to the reputations of his predecessors Grobbelaar and Clemence from the outset, and many of his early errors

James displays the same skill in distributing the ball by hand that Bruce Grobbelaar pioneered before him. The brainstorms that characterised the Zimbabwean's play, however, are thankfully a good deal more rare in his successor's game.

were the products of over-ambition in which that anxiety emerged. Grobbelaar's leaving sent out the clearest of signals that David was now officially recognised as Liverpool's number one, but it still required a public vote of confidence from manager Roy Evans to give him the sense of security he needed to cease trying to outdo the men whose gloves he was bought to fill and begin to develop a goalkeeping identity of his own. James' belief in his latent ability never wavered throughout that time and rather it was his belief in the difficulty of being accepted on his own terms at Anfield that prompted his over-eagerness to impress. Freed of that burden, he gradually evolved his own style over a consistency-building run of more than 100 consecutive matches during the next two seasons, increasingly combining the reliability of Clemence with the acrobatics of Grobbelaar.

The unpredictable brainstorms and headlong rushes from the goal-line that James at first appeared to have picked up from his immediate predecessor were gradually squeezed from his repertoire under the guidance of goalkeeping coach Joe Corrigan, and were replaced by the displays of reflex athleticism that have made him just about the best shot-stopper in the country. At 6ft 5in tall, David has little difficulty in reaching the top corners of his goal, but he can also get down to the feet of his posts with remarkable speed for such a big man, as his record of penalty saves – stopping five of the first eight he faced for Liverpool – points out. Although he finished on the losing side in the 1996 FA Cup final, the Reds keeper displayed the progress he had made in two short years with a virtuoso performance. It did not deserve the cruel irony of seeing him set up Manchester United's winner with his only mistake of the afternoon.

A natural athlete blessed with huge hands, fine co-ordination and pogo-stick spring, James began to add crucial confidence to his long list of goalkeeping attributes as he became one of the most commanding occupiers of the Premiership's penalty boxes and was elevated to the England squad under Glenn Hoddle. He began the 1996-97 season in fine form, conceding just eight goals in an early run of 13 games and keeping all league opposition at bay for almost six hours of football at the turn of the year.

Yet it was within that second spell that things started to turn sour for James. The only flaws still apparent in his make-up at that point were occasional lapses in concentration, a slight weakness in fielding low, bouncing shots close to his body and kicking off the ground that was not the same quality as his efforts out of hand. But a succession of errors during the second half of the season threatened to plunge him into one of the confidence crises that plagued his early Anfield career. A scuffed clearance at Middlesbrough – blamed later on a lapse of concentration caused by eight hours of pre-match computer game playing – sent Liverpool towards an early League Cup exit before James single-handedly surrendered a three-goal lead against Newcastle only for Robbie Fowler to save his blushes in stoppage time. A dropped cross in the next game at Nottingham Forest led to a costly equaliser before the onset of a nightmare spell in which his errors in coming for crosses contributed hugely to his team's departure from the European Cup Winners' Cup and removal from the race for the Premiership through defeats by Manchester United and lowly Coventry.

Roy Evans' wise decision to keep faith with James helped him to finish the season in steadier form, albeit still with something of a question mark hanging over his head. At the tender age of 27, David James has the ability and the opportunity to keep Liverpool's goal in the manner to which it is accustomed for even longer than either Ray Clemence or Bruce Grobbelaar held the fort. To fulfil that promise, he might do well to take a leaf out of the latter man's book when it comes to confidence and bouncing back from mistakes.

Career History
Born: Welwyn, 1 August 1970
Signed: July 1992, from Watford
Full debut: Nottingham Forest 1 Liverpool 0, FA Premiership, 16 August 1992
Games: 207 (one as sub)
Goals: none

International Caps
One England cap

Honours
League Cup 1994-95

Other Club
Watford

David Johnson

Keegan and Toshack, Dalglish and Rush; those were the two striking partnerships that dominated Liverpool's history during the 1970s and 1980s. But between the departure of Keegan and the emergence of Rush there passed a four-year spell in which the Reds continued to accumulate trophies at much the same rate as in the decade on either side. For the latter part of that period at least, they had David Johnson to thank for many of the goals that kept them rolling along the road to glory. A genuine team player, he struck up an instinctive understanding with Dalglish in one of the finest of all Liverpool sides, and had he not been unfortunate enough to have his Anfield career shaded at each end by two of the greatest attackers the British game has seen then he might have provided another addition to that list of classic combinations.

Johnson actually began his career at Everton – and scored a winner for the Blues in a Merseyside derby – before he eventually found his way across Stanley Park, albeit via a three-year stay at Ipswich. Bill Shankly had twice tried to sign him from the Portman Road club and in the end it took a club record £200,000 to incorporate him into the team he had supported as a boy. He was known as 'Johnno' among the Kopites alongside whom he had grown up, and his entire family were such fervent Reds that he actually had a cousin named Ian St John Johnson. When he signed at Anfield during the summer of 1976 his relatives in Halewood threw a street party to celebrate. But his dream move quickly turned into something of a nightmare for the England international as, despite being given a instant debut, he failed to establish himself in the team. With Keegan and Toshack still in their pomp, the new record signing's first season was almost totally overshadowed by their exploits and although his 26 appearances were enough to earn him a Championship medal David became so unsettled by the situation that he demanded a transfer shortly before the start of the 1977-78 campaign. Johnson was the sort of player who needed constant encouragement to instil in him the striker's essential self-belief, and even though by that stage Keegan had left for Hamburg and Toshack was also heading for the exit, the arrival of Kenny Dalglish, coupled with Bob Paisley's tinkering with the idea of playing David Fairclough alongside the Scot, meant he saw little chance of improving his lot and it was only after a move to Leicester City fell through that he steeled himself for the challenge of winning a regular place in the side.

The perfect Liverpool man

On the face of it, Johnno had all the attributes required in a Liverpool striker – he was unselfish, skilful, courageous, tireless in his running, good in the air and had more to his game than just an ability to put the ball in the net – but it was the characteristic that endeared him most to the fans, his determination, that really brought him the breakthrough. Yet in the second half of the 1977-78 campaign, just as he was beginning to show the form that had won him national acclaim at Ipswich, he was struck down with knee ligament damage that forced him to miss the European Cup final. The disappointment of that blow was doubled by the fact that just 12 months earlier he had missed out on the first Champions' Cup triumph after

playing in the FA Cup final defeat by Manchester United, and although his team-mates had him a special winners' medal struck after the victory over Bruges he must have felt that he was destined never to get

David Johnson battles in typically determined fashion against Manchester United's Gordon McQueen in the 1979 FA Cup semi-final. Liverpool lost in a replay, but Johnson soon earned compensation in the shape of his second Championship medal.

his hands on club football's greatest prize. All that changed in Paris three years later, of course, but other successes were quick in coming before that famous win. Johnson's Anfield career really began to take off after the midway point of the 1978-79 season, when 19 starts in the last 20 games of the campaign gave him the opportunity to foster a highly successful partnership with Dalglish. His classic goal-poacher's skills saw him net 16 times in the 30 appearances he made that term and finish runner-up in the First Division scoring charts the following year by returning figures of 21 goals in 37 games. Alongside that recharged striking power in front of goal, Johnno was also making a wider contribution to Liverpool's play in his emergence as an effective foil for the talents of Dalglish, working hard off the ball to draw defenders away from his more skilful partner with perceptive runs into the wider channels and creating openings for the Scot with deftly headed flick-ons and one-touch passes. The pairing reached its zenith in those two seasons, during the first of which Liverpool won the League with a new points record. They wrapped up the Championship once more the following year in appropriate fashion, with two goals from Johnson against Aston Villa sealing overall victory.

David was the fifth postwar player to appear for both Liverpool and Everton, and became the first man to score derby goals in the colours of each club when he struck for the Reds in April 1978. But within 12 months of the 1979-80 Championship success he found himself heading for the situation he had encountered on arriving at Anfield five years earlier, as the threat to his place presented by the progress of Ian Rush loomed ever larger behind him. As if

Always one of the most unselfish of team players, David Johnson's tireless running and the instinctive rapport that he struck up with his striking partner Kenny Dalglish kept the Reds on the trophy trail throughout the second half of the 1970s.

that was not enough, his European Cup final jinx looked to have struck again in the form of a recurrent hamstring problem. That injury ruled him out of the League Cup final before surfacing once more to cost him his place in the replay and two more matches – one in the epic tussle at Bayern Munich – were all he could manage before, in the final league game of the season, finally proving himself ready for Paris. Johnson took such a fearful buffeting from the Real Madrid defence that night that he ended the evening with his shirt torn to shreds. But with Dalglish severely restricted by injury, his willingness to shoulder the extra workload was of massive importance to his side's one-goal win.

Rush had served notice of his talent in Johnno's number nine shirt that season, and the following term made the jersey his own, restricting his rival to just ten starts and a further five appearances as a substitute. One of those run-outs came in the 1982 Milk Cup final, when he gave the fans something to remember him by in pushing through the pass that teed up the last gasp equaliser with which Ronnie Whelan sent the encounter into extra-time. But by then Bob Paisley's decision to use Craig Johnston as a replacement striker had already signalled to Johnson that his time at Anfield was up and he moved back to Goodison for £100,000 in the summer of 1982.

The name of David Johnson may sometimes be lost between those of the Liverpool strikers who preceded and succeeded him, but a stop-gap player was the last thing he ever was and his glory years were among the finest the club has ever known.

Career History

Born: Liverpool, 23 October 1951
Signed: August 1976, from Ipswich Town
Full debut: Liverpool 1 Norwich City 0, Division One, 21 August 1976
Games: 204 (30 as sub)
Goals: 78

International Caps

Eight England caps, six goals

Honours

European Cup 1980-81; League Championship 1976-77, 1978-79, 1979-80, 1981-82; Milk Cup 1981-82

Other Clubs

Everton, Ipswich, Manchester City, Tulsa Roughnecks (USA), Preston North End

Craig Johnston

I f there is such a thing as a model Liverpool player, then Craig Johnston was certainly not it. At a club that prides itself on collective endeavour and where the sacrifice of unconventional individualism has often been seen by outsiders as the price of team success, it wasn't just the quirky Australian's earring and mane of dark curls that marked him out as one of a different breed to the regular Anfield recruit. A hive of buzzing hyperactivity whose non-stop style saw him dubbed 'the headless chicken' by manager Bob Paisley, Craig, sometimes unwisely, always wore his heart on his sleeve, often acted first and thought later and never cared much for what anyone in authority thought about him.

His Liverpool career was punctuated by transfer requests and walkouts, and ended abruptly when he announced that he was leaving after the 1988 FA Cup final to care for his seriously ill sister in Australia, upped sticks and left. That decision was guided by the sense of loyalty and trust in his own emotions that directed all his impulses, from his insistence on missing the first two months of the 1984-85 season to stay with his expectant wife in the Antipodes, to his immediate flight back to Anfield in the aftermath of Hillsborough.

Craig was never really the selfish superstar his behaviour sometimes suggested. Amid the ferocious competition for places the Liverpool squad system generates, a certain degree of self-interest is essential for every hopeful, and once in the starting line-up few players have ever expended as much energy in the cause of their team as Craig Johnston always did. Impetuous, single-minded, stubborn and ambitious to the point of desperation to succeed; he was all those things, but genuinely selfish he was not. The characteristics that define the man also dictated the nature of his game and without them he would not have been half the player who ran his heart out for the red of Liverpool for a full seven years. In fact, without them he would never have become a professional footballer in the first place, for there are few 14 year olds with the determination and willpower to fly halfway around the world in pursuit of the dream that took the young Craig from New South Wales to Teesside, where he had persuaded Middlesbrough to offer him a

Craig Johnston travelled thousands of miles in pursuit of his dream of becoming a professional footballer. That level of commitment became his hallmark during the seven years he spent at Anfield.

three-month trial. Johnston's nascent skills were at first embarrassed in the company he was asking them to keep at Ayresome, but so many hours spent kicking a tennis ball

Johnston's all-action style saw him christened 'the head-less chicken' by manager Bob Paisley, but the pace and enthusiasm that earned him the nickname were the player's greatest assets out on the pitch.

against the stadium wall that they caused him a pelvic strain eventually gave him the technique to match his fitness and stamina.

Those latter qualities, along with his bubbling, boyish enthusiasm for the game and determination to make a name for himself, were always his trump cards, although no one could ever have performed at his breakneck pace without having mastered the highest standards of ball control. Johnston said that he actually slowed his game down after he moved to Liverpool for a club record £650,000 in April 1981, but few who saw him careering around the Anfield pitch like a runaway dodgem car could really have believed it. Craig fell in love with Liverpool almost from the moment he arrived in the city and even decorated the walls of his hotel room with the flags and banners he collected while riding with his new team-mates on the open top bus they used to celebrate winning the European Cup just a few weeks after his transfer. His first taste of action was much longer in coming than that first whiff of glory, and when he was given his chance towards the end of 1981 he suffered initially from an almost inevitable over-eagerness to prove himself that saw him try to do too much on his own, although he wasn't helped by being asked to play out of position as a striker. The crowd, however, loved his colourful style, exuberance and whole-hearted commitment, and he quickly became so popular that Bob Paisley was actually booed by his own crowd for substituting Johnston in a match against Sunderland in March 1982. Craig had his occasional disagreements with the man who signed him as a promising 20 year old but that was nothing compared to the tempestuous relationship he enjoyed with Joe Fagan. Despite later apologising for his part in creating the chasm that existed between the pair, the Australian described Fagan's reign as the most painful and frustrating two years of his life, although ironically it was Joe who gave him his first decent run in his favourite position on the right of midfield.

Lively behaviour

Fagan interpreted Craig's desperate desire to play as suggesting that he believed his needs to be more important than those of the team. Substituted in the drawn 1984 Milk Cup final, Johnston caused a stir by trudging disconsolately away from the arena wrapped in a blanket instead of being presented to the Queen with the rest of the teams; he had to be prevented by his fellow players from walking out on the club after being dropped for a European Cup match at Atletico Bilbao in 1983, and when his contract expired at the end of that season he refused to re-sign until Kenny Dalglish succeeded Fagan.

Forewarned being forearmed, perhaps the new manager had seen enough of Craig while playing alongside him to have a better idea of the best way to handle him than his more traditional predecessor did. No doubt his task was made easier by Johnston's increased willingness to cooperate. The player enjoyed one of his two best seasons with the club as Liverpool took the League and FA Cup double in Dalglish's first term of office. He missed just two of the 63 games the Reds played that season. He had always been quick and skilful but prior to this campaign his darting runs had often lacked purpose, and his fizzing, sodium-on-water performances never had the impact they might have done with better direction. The goal he and all Liverpool fans will always remember best is the one with which he put the Reds into the lead in the 1986 FA Cup final win over Everton, his close-range finish from Rush's cross sending him jumping for joy on the Wembley pitch.

His supreme fitness could not save him from a couple of injuries that limited his contribution in 1986-87, but he returned the following season for his final campaign and one in which his form was as impressive as in the double-winning year. His last appearance for the Reds was as a substitute in the 1988 FA Cup final and Craig kept his promise to quit the game after that match. Back in Australia, surfing in a vest made from his cut-down Liverpool shirt, he has since turned his hand to everything from photography to commentating and from devising TV quiz shows to inventing a revolutionary football boot. He showed as much versatility and determination to make a go of things during his time at Anfield and still stands among the most committed, irrepressible, crowd-pleasing Liverpool servants.

Career History

Born: Johannesburg, 8 December 1960
Signed: April 1981, from Middlesbrough
Full debut: Liverpool 1 Manchester City 3, Division One, 26 December 1981
Games: 259 (36 as sub)
Goals: 39

Honours

European Cup 1983-84; League Championship 1981-82, 1982-83, 1983-84, 1985-86, 1987-88; FA Cup 1985-86; League Cup 1982-83, 1983-84

Other Club

Middlesbrough

Rob Jones

Rob Jones is the bookmakers' friend. In his own way he has made the turf accountants of Merseyside considerably richer over the first five years of his Liverpool career. Backing the defender to score his debut goal for the club has become for Reds fans as habit-forming a weekly gamble as the lottery, and in more than 200 starts their favourite has failed to oblige. While he has struck every piece of Anfield woodwork on several occasions and been foiled by countless acrobatic saves, the ball stubbornly refuses to find its way into the net for him. His shooting is crisp enough – if not always sufficiently accurate – to have earned him at least one appearance on the scoresheet and he does not want for confidence in front of goal; yet until he breaks his duck his finishing prowess will remain a standing dressing-room joke.

Keeping up a fine tradition

Jones may not yet be quite the man to maintain the Liverpool tradition of goalscoring full-backs established by Chris Lawler and Phil Neal, but in every other aspect of his game he is a worthy successor to those two greats. Rob joined the Reds after manager Graeme Souness spotted him playing for Crewe in a match he had attended with the intention of looking at another

player, and £300,000 brought him to the club he had followed as a boy. He arrived in the middle of one of Souness' regular injury crises as a 19 year old and was immediately pitched into action against Manchester United just 48 hours after putting pen to paper at Anfield. Faced with the flying Ryan Giggs, Jones turned in a debut of maturity well beyond his years, demonstrating all the pace, composure and immaculate tackling that had caught his new boss's eye, to help his side to a merited goalless draw.

His subsequent progress was so spectacular that within only 20 games in the top flight he had graduated to the full England side, and he ended the season by collecting an FA Cup winners' medal to go one better in the competition than his grandfather Bill, who was a member of the Liverpool team that lost to Arsenal in the 1950 final. Shin

One of the most impressive England debuts of the 1990s was Rob Jones', against France at Wembley in February 1992. Despite his impressive start in England colours, injury and bad luck disrupted his international career.

splints, the first of a series of injuries that blighted his fledgling international career, forced him to miss out on that summer's European Championships but over the next

Few players have enjoyed such a spectacular rise to fame as Rob Jones. Within eight months of signing from Crewe Alexandra he was an England regular and had collected an FA Cup winners' medal at Wembley.

two years he established himself as the best right-back in the country. He was always a good yard and a half faster than any of his rivals for that title – being unembarrassed by even the very fastest of wingers – and that turn of pace enabled him both to get forward in support of his winger and recover his defensive position in ample time to thwart an opposing attacker. Saddled with a reputation for not being one of the brighter players at the club – his team-mates nicknamed him 'Trigger' after the daftest character in the television comedy programme *Only Fools and Horses* – Rob's footballing brain moves as swiftly as his feet out on the field. His sound positional sense and speed reading of the play have given him the hallmark of quality that shows up in the rarity of his having to make a last-gasp lunging tackle, and his superb balance compensates for his lack of bulk in the challenge.

Despite his early promise, footballing fortune is so fickle a mistress that in mid-1996, at the age of just 24, Rob Jones found himself if not in crisis then certainly at a major crossroads in his career, facing up to the loss of his place with both club and country for up to six months.

more than six months out of action. A susceptibility to illness and injury has always dogged his progress at Anfield and after suffering from recurrent shin splints and a vulnerability to colds and viruses, Rob struggled for the best part of a season with a back problem that left him spending half-time intervals on the treatment table and was only diagnosed as a potentially dangerous fractured vertebra after the 1996 FA Cup final. That scuppered his European Championships hopes and ruled him out of the first half of the following season, although in truth his place in the England line-up had already been jeopardised by, of all things, his fine form for Liverpool.

The defensive system Roy Evans adopted at Anfield in 1994 utilised three centre-halves flanked by two 'wing-backs' charged as much with raiding deep into enemy territory as with guarding their own goal. Jones' pace made him ideal for such a task and although his crossing was not as consistently accurate as it might have been, he played a crucial part in some memorable moves during the early months of the 1995-96 campaign, particularly the Robbie Fowler diving header he picked out against Blackburn Rovers.

During that period, however, Liverpool had not been as effective on the opposite flank and in a bid to restore some attacking balance they brought in new signing Jason McAteer on the right and switched Jones to the left. Beginning the experiment in a grudge match against Manchester United might have been considered a risk, but the Reds tore their rivals to shreds with a performance that was unflattered by a 2-0 winning margin, and the formation remained. However, while McAteer blossomed in his new role to such a degree that it became impossible to omit him from the side, Jones' unfamiliarity with the demands of playing on the left flank began to hit his form and a combination of ill-timed fitness problems and the lost opportunity to impress in his regular position cost him his spot as the England right-back.

Although he admitted his dislike of playing on the left, Jones always performed soundly there. Yet when he returned to fitness after his back problem he struggled to get a game on either flank, managing just three appearances on the right during 1996-97. In his absence, Stig Inge Bjornebye had become a revelation in the left wing-back role, while McAteer's attacking instinct was still preferred on the right. Even in the closing stages of the season when Liverpool reverted to a 4-4-2 formation Jones found new boy Bjorn Tore Kvarme ahead of him in the queue for the right-back berth, sparking rumours of a move to join Kenny Dalglish at Newcastle. Professional that he is, Rob Jones will slot in wherever he is asked to, although memory will remind us that he remains the best right-back in England. How long he must wait before he can prove it again is a different matter altogether.

Career History

Born: Wrexham, 5 November 1971
Signed: October 1991, from Crewe Alexandra
Full debut: Manchester United 0 Liverpool 0, Division One, 6 October 1991
Games: 214 (one as sub)
Goals: none

International Caps

Eight England caps

Honours

FA Cup 1991-92; League Cup 1994-95

Other Club

Crewe Alexandra

Kevin Keegan

At the banquet that followed Liverpool's FA Cup final defeat by Arsenal in 1971, Kevin Keegan ended his first week with the club by announcing to the rest of his table that he was going make his mark at Anfield and become a superstar. His bubbling confidence might have raised a few eyebrows at the time, but after just a few days of pre-season training no one could have doubted the veracity of his prediction for even a second. Although his ball control and basic skills were easily good enough for the highest level it was his determination, enthusiasm and the whole-heartedness that really impressed his new team-mates.

So committed was he in training alone that he once had to be dragged away from squaring up to the enormous Larry Lloyd, while in the 1974 Charity Shield his furious response to a sly right hook from Leeds' Johnny Giles ended with him being the first Englishman to be sent off at Wembley as he and Billy Bremner received their marching orders.

His manager had quickly spotted those battling qualities and he could not believe his luck when it took only £35,000 to prise Kevin away from Scunthorpe United. He joked that he could never return to the town for fear of being arrested for the theft of its team's prize asset. In turn, Shanks made the greatest of impacts on the stocky little 20 year old, who hung on his every word. The Reds boss could see the burning determination that glowed inside his latest signing and knew exactly how to stoke that inner fire to bring out the talent that would make him the finest English centre-forward of the early 1970s.

After just three weeks, Shankly told Keegan that he would play for England; that the player believed him was as much down to his own self-belief as to the source of the prophecy and the conviction with which it was delivered. After his first game, in which he crowned the sort of tire-less, all-action display that would become his trademark with the opening goal of a 3-1 win over Nottingham Forest, finding converts to that view was no longer a problem. Only a little over 12 months later he played the first of his 63 games for his country.

Kevin burst on to the Anfield scene with the most explosive and instant of impacts, and in just the manner that would make him a hero of the Liverpool fans in double-quick time. He had a blistering turn of speed and the skill to keep the ball under control even when travelling at full pelt, but it was the manner in which he applied himself that did

A pre-perm Kevin Keegan looks for space in the Spurs box at Anfield in 1973. The little striker's speed, energy and ability to control the ball while running at pace made him the finest centre-forward of his era.

The great Berti Vogts brings down Kevin Keegan for the penalty that clinched the 1977 European Cup for Liverpool. Afterwards, the German defender turned up at the Reds' hotel to congratulate his tormentor on his magnificent display.

most to win over the judges in the stands. The tousle-haired lad from Doncaster played with the heart of a man twice his size as he fizzed about the pitch with dizzying zest and apparently inexhaustible energy that would see him chasing back into his own half one minute and popping up on his opponents' goal-line the next. He was fearless in the box, could hold the ball up for as long as it took for an opening to appear, combined audacity and certainty in his finishing, and was amazing in the air for someone who stood just 5ft 8in tall.

Twisting and turning as he sped across the ground, Keegan's low centre of gravity and the strength packed into his small frame made him a nightmare to defend against in even the tightest of spaces; a deft little turn and his acceleration would take him clear of his marker and into enough space to rifle in an instant shot. His brain worked as fast as his feet and gave him a priceless gift for producing the unexpected. He didn't enjoy quite the same reputation for mental agility among his team-mates, who nicknamed him Andy McDaft because he was so forgetful and would come out with the silliest of sayings.

An unpopular drinks dispenser

He also surprised his new colleagues on a 1971 end of season trip to Benidorm when, eager to impress, he invited them to a party in his hotel room but caused the gathering to break up after all of ten seconds when he started handing round glasses of lemonade! It was on the field of play that he helped concoct the most potent attacking brew around, through his burgeoning partnership with John Toshack. Although Liverpool drew a rare blank in the combination's first season together, they gelled immediately and went on to terrorise defences across England and Europe for years to come.

Like many great pairings, this duo were thrown together by chance when Shankly tried them out in one of the regular Melwood practice matches the first team played against the reserves. On this occasion the senior side won 5-0, a result that was completely unheard of in such contests, where the second string was desperate to put one over on the 'big heads' and the first-teamers were mainly preoccupied with avoiding injury, and so the coaching staff thought they might be onto something. They certainly were, and as the Reds won seven major trophies in the next five years it was Keegan and Toshack who scored the goals that made them one of the most feared sides on the entire continent. Both players had such an uncanny appreciation of each other's whereabouts that many people actually believed they were psychic.

Roger Hunt scored the goals that took Liverpool out of the Second Division and on to unprecedented success in England and Europe during the mid-1960s. His 41 goals in 41 league games during the 1961-62 season remains a club record.

Ian Callaghan was the most durable servant Liverpool has seen, playing 848 times for the club over 17 years. The arrival at Anfield of tough Scottish striker Ian St John (opposite) marked the beginning of Bill Shankly's red revolution.

One of Liverpool's most memorable European goalscorers in action. Kevin Keegan fires calmly past Mönchengladbach's Gunter Netzer in the 1973 UEFA Cup final.

Another man who often produced the goods in European ties was David Fairclough. Here he heads for glory against Bruges during the Reds' second UEFA Cup final, in 1976.

Tommy Smith (above) gives Liverpool the lead in the 1977 European Cup final. A year later the trophy was retained thanks to Kenny Dalglish's winner against Bruges (opposite above). Phil Neal and Alan Hansen (opposite below) show off the cup.

Alan Kennedy's 1981 European Cup final goal wins big congratulations (opposite top). Graeme Souness beats Real Madrid's Laurie Cunningham in the Paris match (opposite below). Liverpool's third European Cup is displayed by Phil Thompson (above).

Liverpool marked Bob Paisley's final season in charge in a special way: captain Graeme Souness ushered Paisley forward to become the first manager to collect a trophy – the 1982-83 League Cup – at Wembley.

Bruce Grobbelaar saves from Roma's Falcao in the 1984 European Cup final. The goalkeeper's offputting antics in the penalty shoot-out unnerved the Italian spot-kickers and gave his team the chance to win the cup for a fourth time.

Mark Lawrenson dispossesses Everton's Adrian Heath in typically well-timed fashion during the 1984 Milk Cup final, the first time Merseyside's two clubs had met at Wembley. Liverpool won the trophy after a replay.

Phil Neal gives Liverpool the lead in the 1984 European Cup final. Neal is the only Anfield player to have appeared in all five of the club's Champions' Cup final appearances. He scored three times in those games.

Man of the match Steve McManaman skips through the Bolton Wanderers defence en route to scoring the first of his two goals that decided the 1995 Coca Cola Cup final in Liverpool's favour.

John Barnes showed that he was back to his very best when he took on a new midfield role during the 1994-95 League Cup winning season.

Ian Rush, wearing an unfamiliar substitute's jersey, rattles home a swivelling volley to score the winner – and his second goal of the afternoon – in the 3-2 FA Cup final win over Everton in 1989.

Liverpool celebrate their victory in the 1995 Coca Cola Cup final, a win that marked the end of one of the most turbulent periods in the club's history and rounded off a season prior to which they had been tipped to win nothing.

Liverpool's exciting young striker Robbie Fowler, in typically dramatic fashion, dives full length to put Liverpool ahead in the 1996 FA Cup semi-final win over Aston Villa.

Stan Collymore crowns one of Anfield's most memorable nights as he smashes home John Barnes' pass to give the Reds a 4-3 injury-time win over Newcastle United in their April 1996 Premiership match. The £8.5 million striker scored twice and created Liverpool's opener that evening.

The most regular combination the pair put together was a Toshack flick-on giving the onrushing Keegan a shot on goal. While the standard routine yielded many famous strikes, such as the brace Kevin struck in the first leg of the 1973 UEFA Cup final against Borussia Mönchengladbach, the centre-forward would also on occasion scurry out wide to deliver crosses while Steve Heighway took on a more central role in his place. Keegan always reckoned that he scored few spectacular goals because he performed most of his finishing duties inside the six-yard box, but Liverpool fans will remember many emphatic finishes. His predator's instinct surfaced at Wembley in 1974 when he popped up at the far post to slide home Tommy Smith's cross to finish off the FA Cup final win over Newcastle. He had opened the scoring with an exhilarating, accurate volley, and his talent for unexpected innovation displayed itself after just two minutes of the famous 1977 Anfield victory over St Etienne, when he swung in the most audacious of shots from what had looked an impossibly acute angle.

That win was followed by a routine dismissal of FC Zurich which ensured that Kevin Keegan would take his leave of Liverpool in the club's first-ever European Cup final. His move to SV Hamburg of the Bundesliga, for a German record of £500,000, had been sealed some time earlier and the shock of losing their greatest player had taken a slight edge off the affection in which he was held by the Anfield crowd. In Rome that would all be forgotten amid the acclaim that greeted one of his finest displays in the red jersey.

Keegan had scored the goal that won the UEFA Cup in 1976; twelve months later he did not get on the scoresheet, but it was his quicksilver display of unflagging industry and guile that lasted longest in the memory. Borussia Mönchengladbach's German international Berti Vogts had endured a chasing from the little whirlwind in the 1973 UEFA Cup final: he was in for a repeat dose in 1977. Keegan ran him ragged and earned his just reward late in the game by giving the German international the slip near the centre circle and scuttling off towards the Borussia box. Floundering in his slipstream, Vogts lunged desperately at him 12 yards from goal, bringing him down to present the English champions with a clinching penalty.

At Hamburg Keegan was voted European Footballer of the Year twice in succession, a feat previously managed only by the great Johan Cruyff. The honour officially gave him the international superstar status he had vowed to achieve at that dinner in 1971. However, no one who had witnessed his six-year reign as Anfield's king of the Kop required the help of any award to remind them of his true greatness.

Career History

Born: Doncaster, 14 Februray 1951
Signed: May 1971, from Scunthorpe United
Full debut: Liverpool 3 Nottingham Forest 1, Division One, 14 August 1971
Games: 321
Goals: 100

International Caps

63 England caps, 21 goals

Honours

European Cup 1976-77;
UEFA Cup 1972-73, 1975-76;
League Championship 1972-73, 1975-76, 1976-77; FA Cup 1973-74

Other Clubs

Scunthorpe United, SV Hamburg, Southampton, Newcastle United

Alan Kennedy

'Thanks Barney' read the fans' banner the Liverpool players brandished from their open top bus as they toured the city in celebration of the 1981 European Cup triumph. The club would have done well to hang on to that flag as they had good cause, on more than one occasion, to be grateful to the man the Kop called 'Barney Rubble'. Alan Kennedy scored only 21 goals for the Reds in considerably more than 300 matches but almost one fifth of those strikes could be said to have made the most significant of contributions to the winning of four priceless pieces of silverware. His late goal settled the 1981 European Cup final, he tucked away the decisive penalty of the same competition's 1984 edition and also netted vital goals in two League Cup finals into the bargain.

Those figures suggest that the attacking left-back had a keen sense of occasion rather than the most accurate of shots, and that is a verdict the player himself would not dispute. Although he loved nothing better than to charge down the left-wing before letting fly as soon as he was within range of the goal, he once admitted that so many of his hard-hit howitzers had hurtled into the Kop he was surprised that the occupants of the famous terrace did not take to turning up wearing crash helmets.

Power games

The power he packed into his finishing was evident in every facet of his game and it was the determined, battling style in which he rumbled his way around the field that earned him his *Flintstones* cartoon nickname. In that animated series, Barney was always Fred's faithful sidekick, and in a similar manner Kennedy was quite happy to play the grafting role of committed lieutenant to the more obvious star performers of the side. Yet his contribution to the successes of the seven seasons he spent as a first-team regular was recognised as readily by his colleagues as it was by the fans, and was aided in no small measure by his possession of the simple but underrated gift of knowing his own limitations, his strengths and also his

Alan Kennedy hits Liverpool's winning goal in the 1981 European Cup final. The left-back was never a prolific scorer but saved his strikes for the big occasions, netting in two finals of both the Champions' and League Cups.

weaknesses. Not only that, but in light of that knowledge he also had the wit to tailor his game accordingly, accentuating the good points and compensating for the bad.

As far as his all-round game was concerned, the most positive aspect of his footballing make-up was his speed, which both fuelled his swashbuckling raids down the left and gave him the chance to make up lost ground when forced back in defence. That was particularly handy as one of Alan's weaknesses was a tendency to dawdle on his way back from an attack, and he had a quick burst of pace to thank for his late escape from many a sticky situation. Such situations were not unexpected as, having started his career as a winger, Kennedy had a tendency to push forward, although it still took him several seasons to acquire the precise distribution the Anfield system required and demanded. During that time, the wholehearted commitment and determination that so endeared him to the fans were as instrumental as his tidy ball skills in his struggle to establish himself at Liverpool. Robustly built, Kennedy was as firm in the tackle as any top class defender, but what really swung the selection fight his way was the extra attacking option his pace and eye for an opening brought to the side.

Alan Kennedy's rumbustious, rough-and-ready style earned the full-back the Kop nickname of 'Barney Rubble'. Here he brings all his determination to bear in beating Roma's Italian international forward Francesco Graziani in the 1984 European Cup final.

That his greatest attacking coups would come off on the continent might have been hinted at by the omen of his signing for the Reds in Vienna, where the 1978 European Champions were on pre-season tour, because his finest hours were to come in two other great classical cities: Paris and Rome. The most memorable of those magical moments came in the French capital in 1981, when another of what he called 'those crazy runs' of his brought the European Cup back to Anfield for a third time. Liverpool and Real Madrid had spent 83 minutes at the Parc des Princes warily testing and probing each other in a tense tactical contest, until an inspired moment of Barney Rubble directness ended the sparring in the most dramatic fashion imaginable. Chesting down Ray Kennedy's quick throw-in on the left, he avoided a flying tackle from Real's full-back Cortes and burst into the box to unleash a rising, angled drive that flew in at the near post to the surprise of goalkeeper Agustin, who had been expecting a conventional option of a cross. Alan's determination, and the stamina that meant he was still going forward at such a late stage of the game, earned him that goal, and it was the same iron resolution that got him to the final in the first place, for the left-back had broken his wrist in the home leg of the semi-final against Bayern Munich and only played in Paris after deciding to have his plaster removed specially and gamble on a thin bandage protecting it from further damage.

Kennedy had already made more than 100 appearances for the Reds and won the first two of his five Championships by the time of that European Cup triumph, but it was the 1980-81 season the victory crowned which was his most impressive to date. The goal he scored at Wembley, and which appeared to have won Liverpool the League Cup until West Ham forced them to lift the trophy in a replay after levelling in the dying minutes, was largely overlooked in the jubilation his French strike triggered, but he repeated the trick two years later when the pressure was even greater. On that occasion, his side were trailing to Manchester United in the Milk Cup final with time in increasingly short supply. In stepped Barney to stride forward down the left and thump a precious equaliser into the far corner of the tunnel-end goal and set up the extra half-hour in which Ronnie Whelan curled home the winner.

A penalty point

The pressure of that afternoon, however, paled in comparison to the nerve-wracking finale of Kennedy's best Anfield season that unfolded in the penalty shoot-out called upon to settle the 1984 European Cup final in Rome, when it fell to the Wearsider to take the potentially decisive kick. Phil Neal – the Reds' regular expert from the spot – could not bear to watch: Alan had missed the last three penalties he had taken and said that he was more confident of hitting the target from 25 yards than from 12. No one could have guessed that from the confidence with which he converted his effort to join Neal as the only Liverpool player to score in two European Cup finals.

That season proved to be memorable not just for the unprecedented treble that Joe Fagan's side managed to pull off, but also for the fact that Bobby Robson finally heeded the Kop's regular chants of 'Barney for England!' and gave Kennedy his international debut. The following blank campaign proved to be Alan's last at Anfield as by September 1985 Jim Beglin had emerged from the ranks to take his place and prompt him to move on to his native Sunderland. The serious injury that Beglin suffered just 18 months later suggested that Alan Kennedy's departure might have been somewhat premature, but after seven years at the club he had little left to win and absolutely nothing left to prove.

Career History
Born: Sunderland, 31 August 1954
Signed: August 1978, from Newcastle United
Full debut: Liverpool 2 Queen's Park Rangers 1, Division One, 19 August 1978
Games: 349 (two as sub)
Goals: 21

International Caps
Two England caps

Honours
European Cup 1980-81, 1983-84; League Championship 1978-79, 1979-80, 1981-82, 1982-83, 1983-84; League Cup 1980-81, 1981-82, 1982-83, 1983-84

Other Clubs
Newcastle United, Sunderland, Hartlepool United, Beerschot (Belgium), Wigan Athletic, Wrexham

Ray Kennedy

Even in a modern game that rarely finds room for sentiment, the most hard-hearted of observers would have struggled to remain unmoved by the appearance on the pitch of an emotional Ray Kennedy, wracked by Parkinson's Disease, at his 1991 benefit match between Arsenal and Liverpool. The illness had already cost him his career and his health, had ruined his private life and would soon force him to sell his enormous collection of medals to make ends meet. His tearful struggle to greet the fellow greats who had turned out to play for him that day in front of a Highbury crowd of more than 18,000 was touching enough in itself, but the immediate contrast cut by his gaunt figure against the memory of the strong, athletic footballer who had graced the shirts of both sides was the saddest moment of an emotional afternoon. Kennedy was only diagnosed as suffering from Parkinson's in 1987, when he was 35, but had been fighting an unknown battle against the disease for the previous

Kennedy had made his name as a striker in the Arsenal side that won the League and Cup double in 1971, but it was after Liverpool manager Bob Paisley spotted his potential as a midfielder that he earned greatest acclaim.

ten years. To have achieved as much as he did – he left Anfield in 1982 as the only Englishman to have been both a Double-winner and three times European Cup-winner – in the face of such a sapping condition was a true act of sporting heroism.

Ray joined Liverpool on the same July day in 1974 on which Bill Shankly shocked the city by announcing his retirement, which at least distracted much of the attention that a record £180,000 signing might ordinarily have expected to attract. However, he was then left with the worry of wondering whether the new manager, Bob Paisley, would think as highly of him as his predecessor had. The initial answer appeared to be in the negative, for although he scored on his debut it took Kennedy well over a year to establish himself in Paisley's team.

But when he did make the breakthrough and go on to star in some of the club's most successful sides ever, it was the boss he had to thank. The big Geordie had earned a deserved reputation as a talented striker when he helped Arsenal to the Double as a

Graeme Souness and Richard Money are the first to congratulate Ray Kennedy on the 82nd-minute goal in Munich that stunned Bayern and took an injury-hit Liverpool through to their third European Cup final, in 1981.

19 year old in 1971, yet within three years had become so disillusioned with the manner in which that side had been allowed to break up that he wanted out. His unhappiness in his final days as a Gunner saw him put on so much weight that he tipped the Anfield scales at almost 15 stones, a full stone and a half heavier than he had been on his Highbury debut. He returned to peak condition inside his first year with the Reds, but it was a tactical rather than physical change that proved to be the making of him at Liverpool.

The perfect all-round striker

It was Kennedy's standing as one of the best all-round strikers in the country that had set his price so high – he was great in the air, clever on the ground, powerfully built and the owner of a devastating left-foot finish – and although he never lost any of those attributes after his move, Paisley recognised that there was even more to his game than that. Ray had lost much of his appetite for playing up front by the time he came to Liverpool, where Toshack and Keegan were forging the most irresistible forward partnership around, and the knowledge that he had played in midfield as a schoolboy prompted the manager to look for a new role for him.

The dark-haired attacker's skill on the ball, his vision, control and passing ability had already revealed themselves on the training ground, but even Paisley had to admit that he could never have foreseen how successfully they would fit into the left-hand side of his first-team's midfield from the moment he began the experiment in the autumn of 1975. Over the next six years, Kennedy blossomed into one of the finest footballers in Britain and became, in many judges' minds, the player of the 1970s. Demonstrating the great positional sense which convinced his boss that he could even have played at centre-back had the need arisen, he gave his team invaluable width on the left and could open a game up with an instant, telling pass.

A well-balanced character

Aside from his cultured left-foot and confident ball control, he had remarkable balance for such a big man, an attribute that allowed him to stop and turn at pace, while his prodigious strength and powerful frame made him one of the best shielders and protectors of the ball around. He was on occasion susceptible to being turned, but had sufficient tactical nous to allow that to happen only rarely and was always likely to inflict more attacking damage on his opponents than they would on him. He never lost the striker's instincts that fired him to fame, and Bob Paisley always rated him as dangerous inside the box as any player he had ever seen. In fact, the threat Ray posed to opposing goalkeepers was actually heightened by his move into mid-field. He quickly proved himself lethal when arriving from deep to take a pass effortlessly in his stride while moving menacingly into the penalty area. His shooting remained as accurate and powerful as ever, and he came forward to net some vital strikes on a regular basis, never more importantly than in opening the scoring in the 1976 UEFA Cup final and in thumping home the precious away goal that beat Bayern Munich in the European Cup semi-final of 1981.

By that time, although he didn't know it, his illness was beginning to extract its toll on his game. He remembers being transfixed by an involuntarily twitching finger during a derby of the time and could not summon up the energy to remove his shirt after a draining FA Cup tie of the same era. Those were the first signs that something was amiss, but he and the coaching staff jokingly put his increasing tiredness down to encroaching old age. Kennedy also acquired something of a reputation among the fans for laziness, which in retrospect was partly a consequence of the impeccable positional sense that rendered unnecessary the perpetual motion of many a lesser-skilled, high-work-rate player, and partly an indicator of the moment at which Parkinson's first began to slow him down. However, the willingness of the crowd to saddle him with such a tag backed the view of Bob Paisley that Ray was the most underrated of all Liverpool players. The manager believed that his talent was better appreciated on the continent than at home – the consistent Kennedy was just about the most feared of the Reds heroes who regularly conquered Europe – and that his true value was only recognised in the absence of his powerhouse presence from the midfield. Paisley was just as frustrated by the defensive role Ray was asked to play for England, which largely negated his creative talents and so frustrated the player that he retired from the international scene in 1981, declaring that he felt more pride in pulling on the shirt of his club than his country.

The volatile virtuoso

That outburst was typical of Kennedy's volatile off-field temperament and many who knew him were surprised by the transformation that came over him as soon as he crossed the touchline. During a match he could control his emotions impeccably even under the most extreme provocation, whereas in training he was touchy and short-fused, and had a tendency towards waywardness away from the club, occasionally coming to blows with even his chief partner-in-crime, Jimmy Case. The onset of his undiagnosed illness could not have helped those moods, as his growing sense of having something wrong with him but never being able to put a finger on the cause of the problem left him increasingly frustrated. And it may too have ultimately ended his Liverpool career by bringing about the two sendings off that allowed Ronnie Whelan to claim his place during Ray's suspension in 1981.

He moved on to John Toshack's Swansea in January 1982, but he was already on the downward path that would lead eventually to the doctor's appointment five years later at which his condition was finally recognised. The hardships that followed have left him facing a more formidable opponent than any of those he ever came up against on the field of play.

Ray Kennedy may often have been underrated by many among the Liverpool crowd, but in his eight years at the club he proved himself one of his country's finest players. A benefit match at Anfield would be as fine a way as any to show him the belated appreciation his talent deserved.

Career History
Born: Seaton Delaval, Co Durham, 28 July 1951
Signed: July 1974, from Arsenal
Full debut: Chelsea 0 Liverpool 3, Division One, 31 August 1974
Games: 384 (three as sub)
Goals: 72

International Caps
17 England caps, three goals

Honours
European Cup 1976-77, 1977-78, 1980-81; UEFA Cup 1975-76; League Championship 1975-76, 1976-77, 1978-79, 1979-80, 1980-81; League Cup 1980-81

Other Clubs
Arsenal, Swansea City, Hartlepool United

Chris Lawler

He was 'The Silent Knight', 'The Red Ghost of Anfield', even 'The Creeper'; and in their own way, each of Chris Lawler's nicknames summed up his singular style and character. The Kop handed him the first of those monikers in tribute to his modest gallantry, while room-mate Tommy Smith and manager Bill Shankly coined the latter two in summing up the way he would sneak forward unnoticed from full-back to appear from apparently nowhere in the opposition box at precisely the moment of maximum danger. The nature of those tags also reflected the quiet manner for which Chris was known both on and off the field. He was the most phlegmatic of players, who met the twin imposters of triumph and disaster with the same unflickering absence of emotion. Those who knew him away from the pitch found him warm and witty company, yet had to admit that while never shy he was unmistakably the quiet type. Smith, whose friendship with Lawler dates from their time together in the Liverpool Boys side, always reckoned that he had done well to get anything more than a 'yes' or a 'no' out of his mate, while the full-back's reticence – perhaps the legacy of growing up struggling to get a word in edgeways as one of 13 children – was also the source of one of the more famous Bill Shankly anecdotes. The manager once turned to the unshakeably honest Lawler to resolve the matter of a disputed goal in one of his fiercely contested five-a-sides, but when Chris' verdict failed to support his case, Shankly spluttered back: 'All these years you've been here you've never said a word, and now when you do speak it's to tell a lie!'

Chris Lawler went about his business in the quietest of manners and with the least possible fuss, but his talent was always impossible to overlook. He represented England at every level and played 546 times for his club.

Quiet brilliance

A quiet man he may have been, but Lawler's record fairly screams out his brilliance. Captain of England Schoolboys, he went on to represent his country at every level, was the first Division One full-back to score more than 50 goals without the aid of penalties, scored on his international debut and played 316 consecutive matches for Liverpool between October 1965 and May 1971, a run that was only ended by the resting of the entire first team before that season's FA Cup final. Those are the statistics, but as ever they tell little about the style with which he accomplished those deeds. Although he spent almost his entire Anfield career at right-back – he deputised occasionally in his earlier years for Ron Yeats at centre-back – Chris possessed all the ball skills of a top

Lawler was the first full-back to score 50 goals in the top flight without the aid of penalties. Here he shows all his shooting skill in volleying towards the Borussia Mönchengladbach goal in the UEFA Cup final of 1973.

midfielder and was comfortable in every area of the pitch. He always remained cool, calm and cultured in his play, no matter how much pressure he faced, and in this respect comparisons with the great Franz Beckenbauer were by no means far fetched.

Lawler's reading of the play meant that he rarely found himself in difficulties and on the few occasions he did, the classy defender had the confidence and ability to play his way out of trouble and was as adept at starting off constructive movements for his own side as he was at breaking up those of the opposition.

The art of perfect timing

It was the regularity with which he finished off such attacking moves, however, that really caught the eye, although it was generally only as he was putting the ball into the back of the net that his presence in the penalty area was first noticed. His astonishing scoring record made opponents well aware of the danger he posed to their goal, yet still they could not pick him up. Timing and anticipation were the keys to Chris's art, aided and abetted by his fine footballing brain. Many of his strikes, few of which came from outside the box, arose from his instinct for finding unattended space within sight of the posts. Just as great a number could be attributed to the sharp eye for an opening his all-round vision gifted him. Lawler followed play stealthily from full-back, always looking to advance down the right flank into unguarded space created by a move developing down the other side of the pitch, ready to pounce on any weakness or opening the instant it presented itself. The far post was his favourite and best-stocked hunting ground, and of all the goals he poached in that area the most remembered is probably the one that clinched a 1970 Anfield derby win in which Liverpool came from 2-0 down to snatch victory at the death. John Toshack won a high cross in the air with just a few minutes of the match remaining and found Chris galloping on to his flick to rifle home the winner from beyond the far upright.

Born in Norris Green, Lawler joined the Anfield groundstaff as a 15 year old in 1959. At that age he was already 5ft 11in tall and weighed 11st 6lb, a build that had contributed to the name he had already made for himself as a talented centre-half. He made his League debut against West Bromwich Albion in March 1963 and a few weeks later turned in an impressive performance in the Reds' FA Cup semi-final defeat by bogey team Leicester City. Two seasons later, Gerry Byrne's switch from the right of defence to the left in place of Ronnie Moran let Chris in at full-back, a position he had swiftly mastered after reaching the conclusion that the presence of Ron Yeats at centre-half would severely limit his opportunities in that role. Lawler never looked back and was a permanent fixture in the side for the better part of a decade. Having grown to six feet tall, he was a handful in the air at both ends of the pitch, and although never blessed with explosive speed off the mark he compensated in sufficient other ways to remain unruffled by the pace of Albert Johannson in the 1965 FA Cup final.

A permanent fixture

Chris added another medal, this time a League Championship, in only his second full season as he embarked on the run of consistency that saw him miss only that one pre-Cup final match in over 350 Liverpool fixtures until November 1973, when he suffered a knee injury at Queens Park Rangers. Sadly that first serious injury, which required cartilage surgery, was also to be his last as it effectively finished off his Anfield career. Out of the game for the better part of a whole season, the tall full-back was only a shadow of his former self on his return, and he moved on to Portsmouth during 1975. As was his nature, Chris left quietly and without any fuss. His outstanding record, however, ensured that his departure went anything but unnoticed.

Career History

Born: Liverpool, 20 October 1943
Signed: October 1960
Full debut: Liverpool 2 West Bromwich Albion 2, Division One, 20 March 1963
Games: 546
Goals: 61

International Caps

Four England caps, one goal

Honours

UEFA Cup 1972-73; League Championship 1965-66, 1972-73; FA Cup 1964-65

Other Clubs

Portsmouth, Stockport County

Tommy Lawrence

The Anfield crowd knew him as 'The Flying Pig' and a newspaper report of 1970 described him as 'one of football's tubbiest goalkeepers'. Yet the occasional ribbing that Tommy Lawrence took over his physique was never anything but affectionate and stopped the instant his ability came under discussion. In fairness, the newspaper piece was actually praising the new slimline figure he unveiled at the start of the 1970-71 season in an ultimately vain attempt to regain his place from Ray Clemence. And the 14 stones he had weighed in at for the previous campaign was not entirely unheard of among the league's custodians. Having one of the sport's most evocative nicknames, however, counted against Tommy in the final reckoning. It endeared him to the supporters but overshadowed his professional exploits.

Tommy Lawrence was the first in a long line of great Liverpool goalkeepers of the modern era, and was the first custodian regularly to act as a sweeper who would venture outside his box to provide extra cover behind his defence.

Lawrence, who joined the club as an amateur after impressing in a junior trial match, remains one of Liverpool's most underrated keepers and it is no coincidence that both he and his illustrious successor shared many of the same attributes. Tommy was still good enough in the late 1960s to keep Clemence out of the team for two and a half seasons and during that period the new boy could – and surely did – learn much from watching the man he was asked to understudy. An easy-going, undemonstrative character whose preferred destination for his summer break was always a holiday camp in North Wales, Lawrence was among the least flashy and most consistent of goalies. He could always be relied upon to perform sensibly and do the simple things well, and to that solid base he could add the qualities of concentration, bravery, good reflexes and fine positional awareness.

A master of concentration

Like Clemence, he possessed the priceless ability to pull off outstanding saves after having gone long periods of the game without a touch of the ball: Tommy was often dubbed Anfield's 'first spectator', playing behind a solid defence that protected him as well as any in the country. And for a man of his proportions – he was squarely built but no giant at 5ft 11in – he protected his goal with remarkable agility. He allowed the aerial strength of Ron Yeats to deal with the majority of crosses that flew into their penalty box, and in return began the Liverpool tradition of goalkeepers who act as sweepers when their back four is pushing up. His clear reading of the play gave him the early warning he needed to cover enough ground to be in a position to avert the danger, as often as not by throwing himself courageously upon the toecaps of his onrushing opponent.

Scotland international goalkeeper Tommy Lawrence was heavily built and was not the tallest of goalkeepers, but his lithe athleticism between the posts belied his solid physique and earned him a reputation as one of the finest keepers around.

A calf injury that forced him to miss only his fifth game in seven and a half seasons – an FA Cup tie at Wrexham in January 1970 – essentially ended his Anfield career by allowing Clemence to stake his claim to a regular first-team place. Almost exactly the same situation had given Lawrence his chance back in 1962. Jim Furnell, who had helped the Reds to the Second Division title the previous term, damaged a finger in training and so handed Tommy promotion after five years of playing for the reserves and the A team. Furnell had been in fine form prior to his mishap but his replacement's impressive debut against West Brom, followed up by just as fine a display at Burnley, was enough to persuade Bill Shankly to keep faith with the 22 year old. The ousted keeper's subsequent quick departure to Arsenal then freed Lawrence to open his record of enviable consistency, as he missed just three matches in his first four seasons. That FA Cup-winning campaign of 1964-65 ended with Tommy having thrice to retrieve the ball from the back of his smoke- and firework-filled net at San Siro as Inter Milan overturned the two-goal European Cup deficit Liverpool had inflicted upon them in the semi-final's first-leg.

The Italians' aggregate winner was unstoppable but they had broken their own golden rule of never challenging the keeper when Peiro kicked the ball out of Lawrence's grasp to level the tie. The big goalie could have been faulted for giving him the chance to do so as he bounced the ball out towards the edge of his area. Such criticism, however, would have been churlish in the extreme for it was Tommy whom the Reds had to thank in large part for getting as far as the semi-final in the first place by pulling off two world-class saves to keep the first leg of the previous round goalless in Cologne.

A strong, powerful man, Lawrence enjoyed more success on the domestic stage than at international level with either club or country. He won only three caps for Scotland and it was at his own national stadium, Hampden Park, that Liverpool suffered their agonising extra-time defeat by Borussia Dortmund in the final of the 1965-66 European Cup-Winners' Cup. That blow was softened by the second League Championship of Tommy's career, sewn up before the team travelled to Glasgow, but by the time the trophy next returned to Anfield he had moved on to Tranmere Rovers, crossing the Mersey in October 1971.

Tommy had, however, left one mark by which the record books could remember his outstanding contribution, for fewest league goals conceded in a season. Liverpool set that record in 1968-69 and it could never have been achieved without his reliable presence between the sticks. It is altogether fitting that the only goalkeeper ever to better that record is Ray Clemence, the man who learned so much from the example that Tommy Lawrence set.

Career History

Born: Dailly, Ayrshire, 14 May 1940
Signed: October 1957
Full debut: West Bromwich Albion 1 Liverpool 0, Division One, 27 October 1962
Games: 387
Goals: none

International Caps

Three Scotland caps

Honours

League Championship 1963-64, 1965-66; FA Cup 1964-65

Other Club

Tranmere Rovers

Mark Lawrenson

Any footballer who plays alongside Alan Hansen and does not suffer by comparison must be quite a performer. Fortunately for Liverpool Football Club, for seven success-strewn seasons in the 1980s, Mark Lawrenson was that man. Perhaps as a result of regular humblings on the international stage, the British tend to shy away from classing any of their stars as among the best in the world. But as a club level centre-back pairing, Lawrenson and Hansen could not unreasonably be said to have had few equals in either the global game of their era or the entire history of domestic football. Their names are as synonymous with the Reds' finest defences as are Keegan and Toshack or Dalglish and Rush with the team's most potent attacks. Both players were genuinely world class and once their talents had been combined they presented an almost immovable obstacle for their opponents. The image of Hansen striding imperiously out of defence with the ball at his feet may be the public's most enduring memory of the partnership, but in all other areas Lawrenson was at least the equal of his colleague. Although he never ran with quite the flowing grace of the tall Scot, the Republic of Ireland international was deceptively quick over the ground and, allied to excellent anticipation and awareness, that pace meant there were very few forwards who could escape his attentions for long.

Stretching exercises

And even on those rare moments when all did appear to be lost, Mark would demonstrate the skill that made him the finest and cleanest recovery tackler in the country, stretching out a long, willowy leg to reclaim the ball from the attacker's toe before calmly rising to touch the ball on to Hansen or bring it away from the danger zone himself. He was a powerful challenger in head-to-head confrontations as well, but it was the impeccably timed, elastic elegance of his later interventions for which he was best known.

Lawrenson had initially made a name for himself at Brighton and Hove Albion, where he won his first international honours. It took a club record £900,000 to persuade the Seagulls to part with their prize asset in the summer of 1981. The acquisition of the 24 year old was in some quarters considered an

Mark Lawrenson's Liverpool career was cut short by a serious achilles tendon injury, but his cool, intelligent and skilful brand of defending had already assured him of his lasting place among Anfield's greatest players.

unusual and unnecessary step, for in Alan Hansen and Phil Thompson the Reds already possessed a central defence that was the envy of the Football League. In signing Mark, Bob Paisley demonstrated once again his foresight and concern to map out the club's future.

The spare, leggy defender played only three reserve games in his entire Anfield career: an injury to Alan Kennedy gave him his chance in the very first game of the 1981-82 campaign. After standing in for the Wearsider at left-back, he moved to centre-half when similar fitness problems forced out Phil Thompson in the New Year. By the end of the season he had also filled in on the left of midfield and had even deputised for Graeme Souness in the centre of the pitch for a spell. It wasn't much longer before he had played in every outfield position in the side. He performed so outstandingly in each of those roles that as Liverpool cruised to the title in April 1982 the manager singled out Mark as his player of the year, citing him as the team's 'most consistent player in every position he operated in'. Paisley was also impressed with the attitude of his new signing towards the varied tasks he was handed, for he never gave anything less than his very best in whatever number shirt he was asked to wear. The boss could, though, have picked any of a whole host of attributes to admire, for Lawrenson was one of the finest all-rounders in the game. Tall and strong in the air, he was also instantly at home with the Reds' passing and movement; his control was slick and his distribution both intelligent and reliable. Those qualities were the perfect complement to the skills of Hansen in the centre of the Liverpool back line, and when a serious injury to Phil Thompson four months

Lawrenson's all-round ability allowed him to slot into any of the outfield positions, because as well as being just about the best recovery tackler in the game his vision and distribution made him an impressive creator as well.

into the 1982-83 season brought them together on a long-term basis, one of the finest defensive partnerships seen on these shores was born.

The silver-winning spree the side embarked upon, winning two trophies that term and the unprecedented treble of League, European Cup and League Cup the next year, owed much to the reassuring security the elegant duo provided. In that 1984 final of the Champions' Cup it was Mark's mastery of Roma's attack during a tense second half that saw Liverpool through to the penalty shoot-out in which they triumphed. That side's success in almost every competition they entered shows up in the fact that in those first three seasons, Lawrenson played in a stamina-testing 58, 54 and 65 matches. The half-century of appearances was topped again in 1985-86 as the Reds wrapped up the League and FA Cup double. The irresistible football played in the 6-0 hammering of Oxford United, on the same March afternoon that title rivals Everton slipped up at Luton, signalled that the Championship was really on, but the price of that confirmation was an injury to the elegant number four. Gary Gillespie was brought in and a string of solid performances appeared to have assured him of his Cup final place, only for sudden illness to allow Mark to slot seamlessly back into the team with a typically cultured display.

Bad hair days

That Liverpool side of Lawrenson's finest years enjoyed so much success that the player could later look back and genuinely say that virtually the only thing that he would ever have changed about his time at Anfield was the misguided set of highlights that he wore in his hair in 1985.

But if trouble with his hair – it was also set alight by a stray firework during the previous season's European Cup semi-final in Bucharest – was his only problem during those early days, then he found a lot more on his plate in the second half of his Anfield career as injury hit him hard. A dislocated shoulder had almost cost him a European Cup final appearance at Heysel and a hairline shin fracture threatened his Double chances 12 months later, but Mark had been an infrequent visitor to the treatment room until his achilles tendon ruptured in the course of a home match against Wimbledon in March 1987.

That injury sapped much of mcuh of his pace and after a couple of aborted comebacks he had to admit defeat and limped out of top-class action for good. Liverpool have proved time and time again that no player is ever irreplaceable, but few losses have been felt more keenly than the premature departure of Mark Lawrenson.

Career History

Born: Preston, 2 June 1957
Signed: August 1981, from Brighton and Hove Albion
Full debut: Wolves 1 Liverpool 0, Division One, 29 August 1981
Games: 341 (nine as sub)
Goals: 17

International Caps

38 Republic of Ireland caps, five goals

Honours

European Cup 1983-84; League Championship 1981-82, 1982-83, 1983-84, 1985-86, 1987-88; FA Cup 1985-86; League Cup 1981-82, 1982-83, 1983-84

Other Clubs

Preston North End, Brighton and Hove Albion

Sammy Lee

There are not many Liverpool players who have stood smaller in stature than Sammy Lee, but there are even fewer who were ever bigger of heart. For whatever the Reds' pocket battleship lacked in inches he more than made up for with the fierce commitment and dynamic enthusiasm that helped his side to ten major honours in his five full seasons as a first-team regular.

Like Jimmy Case, the man he replaced on the right of the Reds' midfield at the start of the 1980s, Lee was a lad from the south end of the city who had grown up on the Kop dreaming of playing for the club he adored. Taken on as a 16 year old, the 5ft 4in school-leaver was given more chance of making the grade than most: he was still in the reserves when Bob Paisley touted him in public as the next Ian Callaghan. The manager admitted that he didn't quite have Cally's 'nip' of acceleration, but in his faultless character, vision, passing and knowledge of the game he was a worthy successor to the great midfielder. He certainly had all the dedication and determination that would be expected of any Callaghan clone. When selected for his first mini-derby in December 1976, he insisted on still turning out with his regular team-mates in the Liverpool youth side 24 hours beforehand. And breaking into the strongest midfield in the country was as much a triumph of single-mindedness as of skill.

Lee only ever grew to 5ft 7in, but his manager never saw that lack of height as anything of a problem for him, perhaps remembering his own playing career as the tough, stocky little wing-half that many observers saw more than a trace of in young Sammy's make-up. Paisley had enough faith in the chunky midfielder to begin naming him as first-team substitute before he had reached 19, although it was two months after that birthday that he finally got into the action proper.

No wonder Sammy Lee is smiling: the 5ft 7in tall midfielder has just given Liverpool a vital lead in their 1984 European Cup semi-final against Dinamo Bucharest with the rarest of headers.

Debut day

An injury to David Johnson after just seven minutes gave him his chance in a home game against Leicester City during April 1978. The teenager marked that debut with a goal, albeit not the most spectacular one he ever scored, as visiting keeper Mark Wallington allowed his half-hit effort to trickle through his legs and into the net. Case's continuing excellence limited Sammy to occasional appearances for the remainder of the decade, and it was not until early on in the 1980-81 campaign that the irrepressible understudy's perseverance paid off and he was given the chance to make the number eight shirt his own. Lee did just that, and missed only a handful of matches over the next four seasons, accumulating a stack of honours in the process.

Energetic excellence

Blessed with a solid physique and excellent all-round vision, Sammy slotted seamlessly into the right side of the Reds' midfield, forging a fine partnership with his full-back Phil Neal. His tackling and positional sense allowed him to cover for Neal whenever he set off on one of his sorties into enemy territory, and his own energetic support play was an integral part of Liverpool's attacking strategy. That unselfish, tireless commitment is what he is best remembered for, and the amount of ground he covered was quite phenomenal – in the words of team-mate Alan Kennedy: 'If he hadn't done so much running, he would have been about six foot three!'

His goals return does not reveal it, but Lee was also the owner of a cannonball shot. The current Reds reserve team coach scored only 19 times in his entire Anfield career, but two of those strikes at least gave him something to talk to Joe Corrigan about when the former Manchester City star joined the backroom staff as goalkeeping coach in 1994. The conversation may have been a rather one-way affair, however, as successive visits to Maine Road in 1980-81 and 1981-82 saw Sammy beat big Joe with a 30-yard free-kick and a 25-yard pile-driver. Another vital finish came from the most unlikely of sources to give Liverpool a first-leg lead over Dinamo Bucharest in the semi-final of the 1984 European Cup, as Lee

Lee's goalscoring return for the Reds was only ever a modest one, but the little right-footer had one of the most powerful shots around, and a high proportion of his strikes came from spectacular long-range efforts.

somehow out-jumped the Romanian defence to head cleanly into the Anfield Road end goal. The diminutive midfielder scored three other goals in the European Cup, a competition in which he was a winner twice and for which he reserved some of his finest performances, particularly when his team were up against it. Liverpool had been frustrated by Dinamo before Sammy struck with his header to put a different complexion on the tie, and he turned in a superb defensive performance in that year's final when the Reds had to dig deep for long periods to deny Roma on their own pitch. But it was the 1981 Champions' Cup triumph that saw his most memorable European display, in the nail-biting semi-final clash with Bayern Munich. A 0-0 draw at Anfield had made the Germans hot favourites to progress but their over-confident approach to the return leg – they even printed ticket details for the final in the match programme – roused an injury-ravaged Liverpool into arguably their finest effort abroad to win through by Ray Kennedy's priceless away goal. And no one turned in a more tenacious, battling performance than Sammy Lee, who doggedly man-marked Bayern's dangerous Paul Breitner out of the game, denying him any meaningful sort of kick and making him pay for his first-leg comment that Liverpool's football lacked intelligence.

Those European Cup successes stood at either end of a three-year spell in which Liverpool won three League Championships and as many League Cups. Lee was a key member of all those sides. As a lover of old Hollywood movies, Sammy was quite at home with a happy ending, but found that his own Anfield career was not to finish on an upbeat note. After being ever-present in the 1983-84 treble-winning team he suffered an inexplicable loss of form the following term that was then compounded by slow-healing injuries.

He began the 1985-86 campaign partnering Jan Molby in the centre of the Liverpool midfield, Craig Johnston having now muscled in on the right-sided berth. But the signing of Steve McMahon in September effectively brought down the curtain on Sammy Lee's days as a Liverpool player. He made enough appearances for the side during that term to qualify for his fourth Championship medal, but in August 1986 he set off on a journey that would take him to Queens Park Rangers, Spanish side Osasuna, Southampton and Bolton Wanderers before finally bringing him back to his beloved Reds to coach the second team from June 1992.

That the club was so keen to put its future stars in his hands is the clearest of indicators that Sammy Lee's footballing habits were always of the very highest Anfield order.

Career History

Born: Liverpool, 7 February 1959
Signed: April 1976
Full debut: Southampton 1 Liverpool 1, Division One, 24 April 1979
Games: 286 (seven as sub)
Goals: 19

International Caps

14 England caps, two goals

Honours

European Cup 1980-81, 1983-84; League Championship 1981-82, 1982-83, 1983-84, 1985-86; League Cup 1980-81, 1981-82, 1982-83, 1983-84

Other Clubs

Queens Park Rangers, Osasuna, Southampton, Bolton Wanderers

Billy Liddell

As renowned as Liverpool are for shrewd shopping in the transfer market, they can have struck few better bargains than the one that brought Billy Liddell to Anfield in 1938. The £200 donation that persuaded Scottish junior side Lochgelly Violet to part with the then 17 year old bought the Reds not only a man who would become one of the finest players in their history but also a truly heroic figure more deserving of his status as a footballing legend than almost any other bearer of the title.

Both on the field and off it, Billy Liddell always lived up to the very highest of standards and was an example and inspiration to all. A supreme athlete, he was one of the most complete players of his day and to many seasoned observers is still the greatest performer the club has seen. Away from the game he did a vast amount of voluntary work for local boys' clubs and after his retirement he became a magistrate, a lay preacher and bursar of Liverpool University. The selflessness and sense of duty that guided his life outside football was as central to his approach as his vocation itself, and he was never anything less than a model professional. It was his misfortune that, for the greater part of his two decades at Anfield, there were too few other players of his ability at the club. The most modest of men, Liddell would deny that he was forced to carry the team by himself for long periods of his career, but the fact that his side was universally known by the nickname 'Liddellpool' provides the most telling measure of his influence.

Wartime heroics

Signing professional in 1939 – a full nine months after he arrived from Scotland to join the staff at just 16 – meant the first six years of his senior Anfield career coincided with World War II, in which he served as a navigator with the RAF, but throughout that time he managed to play regularly in regional competition for his new club. His talent on either flank, or in the centre-forward position where his heading ability and courage stood out, was instantly obvious and soon confirmed by a hat-trick against Manchester City

So important to the Reds' cause was the great Billy Liddell that the team was known throughout the land as 'Liddellpool'. Although best known as a winger, Liddell still occupies fourth place in the Anfield scoring charts.

Liddell evades a clutch of English tacklers while playing for Scotland at Wembley in 1953. His decision to play his football south of the border cost him the chance to win more than the 28 caps he was awarded.

legend Frank Swift. Liddell's skill and dedication also brought him to the attention of his national selectors, but the latter of those attributes almost cost him his first cap. Picked on the advice of Matt Busby for a 1942 match against England, the flying winger insisted on turning out for Liverpool's A team a week beforehand in order to keep himself fit. But after just five minutes, and before he had even touched the ball, a clash of heads with an opposing defender saw him carried from the field with concussion and a badly split lip to spend the next 10 days in hospital. Fortunately for Billy, the international was postponed because of bad weather and he was fit to take his place in the rearranged fixture, scoring once himself and helping team-mate Jock Dodd to another three in a 5-4 win.

Liddell won 28 peacetime caps for Scotland, a figure that does little justice to his dashing skills. A fairer indicator of his standing on the international stage is his status as one of only two players – Stanley Matthews being the other – chosen to appear in both Great Britain sides that faced the Rest of Europe and the Rest of the World in 1947. Billy's modest international career was handsomely compensated for by the adulation he earned in front of the Kop. Once the war was over, a full debut hat-trick showed that the powerful outside-left intended wasting little time in making his presence felt and although Albert Stubbins scored the goals that won the 1946-47 Championship he never hid the fact that the vast majority of his chances were carved out for him by Liddell.

Shooting and scoring power

Yet so well-rounded was his entire game that Billy was much more than just a creator, as his 229 goals – the fourth highest total in Liverpool history – and his position as top scorer in all but one of nine seasons during the 1950s readily testify. For the Scottish winger was blessed with a shot as searing as his pace, once striking the ball so powerfully against the goal frame being guarded by club-mate Cyril Sidlow in a Hampden international that the Liverpool and Wales keeper was convinced that the upright would break!

The rest of Liddell's play was as powerful as his shooting, for his solid, muscular frame made him a handful for even the most physical of opponents. Indeed, so strong was the man from the Fife mining village of Townhill that he was often at his best in the worst of conditions, striding clear through clinging mud and hitting the soggy ball prodigious distances that others would struggle to match in the dry, particularly from corner kicks, which he was able to land accurately at the far post in all weathers. Those passes he delivered from the flanks, whether at set-pieces or in open play, were Billy's speciality and were feared for their pace, precision and unpredictable variety by every defence he faced. His favoured approach to a shooting chance was to come tearing down the left-wing at opponents before cutting inside to let fly at the target, but he was equally at home with the ball on either foot – hence his ability to shine on both sides of the pitch – and would torture defenders with his footwork just as soon as go past them with his sprinter's speed and boxer's strength.

He demonstrated his supreme balance and lightning reflexes on countless occasions, including one particular gale-lashed Anfield encounter with Preston North End. After struggling to keep the ball on one spot at a free-kick while he stepped back to measure his run-up, Liddell eventually moved forward to strike it right-footed. But as he was about to connect, the ball started to roll away in the wind. Without so much as breaking stride, Billy instantly altered his approach to shift his weight from one foot to the other and thumped an unstoppable left-foot shot into the net.

Leading the way to the final

During 1950, Liddell's goals put Liverpool into the semi-final and then the final of the FA Cup, but at Wembley he was unable to add to his medal collection as the Reds went down 2-0 to Arsenal. After that defeat, the team began to go into decline and even Billy's individual brilliance and bravery could not prevent them from dropping out of the top flight. Yet he reacted to that disappointment in typical fashion, continuing to perform with all the verve and commitment that had characterised his efforts in the more glamorous arena of Division One, scoring on average once every one and a half matches. Such a record suggests that age placed no limit on his genius, for the modest hero was 32 when Liverpool were relegated. That was true up to a point, for as time went by he compensated for an inevitable loss of pace by developing his passing skills from a deeper position in midfield.

With each succeeding season the task of trying to haul the Reds to promotion grew tougher and tougher, and when Billy finally decided to hang up his boots in 1960 the Anfield side were still stranded in the Second Division. It took another Scot, Bill Shankly, to restore them to the top flight, but the exploits of Billy Liddell throughout the 21 years that he devoted to Liverpool Football Club show that greatness should not always be measured by the contents of a player's trophy cabinet.

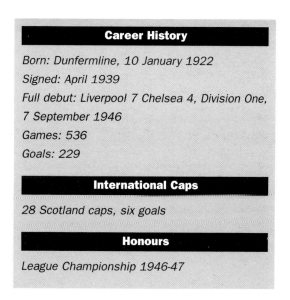

Career History

Born: Dunfermline, 10 January 1922
Signed: April 1939
Full debut: Liverpool 7 Chelsea 4, Division One,
7 September 1946
Games: 536
Goals: 229

International Caps

28 Scotland caps, six goals

Honours

League Championship 1946-47

Alec Lindsay

Alec Lindsay's left foot, believed Bill Shankly, could strike a ball as sweetly as 'a mashie niblick by Jack Nicklaus'. Shanks had little time for golf but knew enough about the game to recognise that the comparison between his blond-haired full-back's sweetly flighted passes and the Golden Bear's precise approach-play with the six iron was not an idle one. While most defenders of the time cleared their lines with all the subtlety of a driver on a pitch and putt course, Lindsay's fluid stroke through the ball floated it gently to the flag stick of his waiting forwards, and for much of the first half of the 1970s his distribution skills gave Liverpool an attacking option to complement the raiding of Chris Lawler on the opposite flank.

The former Bury man's passing ability had been obvious from even the days before he arrived at Anfield in March 1969, as legend has it that Shankly actually went to Gigg Lane to watch another player but returned home with the more impressive Lindsay. However, a dispute over whether his talents would be better employed in attack or defence almost ended his career with the Reds before it had really begun. The burly Lancastrian had been operating as a wing-half in the Shakers' midfield before a £65,000 transfer deal took him to Liverpool, where he found himself pushed even further forward. His traditional year's apprenticeship in the reserves saw him employed as a striker, and the unmatched 22-goal haul that fired the team to the Central League title suggested that Shankly had pulled off another master-stroke.

Alec Lindsay's Anfield career almost ended before it had begun when he demanded a transfer after a row with manager Bill Shankly over his best position. A sudden chance to play at left-back, however, settled the argument and Lindsay never looked back.

A further two goals in his first two senior games – in a 10-0 Fairs Cup mauling of little Dundalk and a 2-2 League draw at Ipswich in October 1969 – appeared to confirm that opinion, although the player himself was not at all happy with the situation as he preferred to operate in the more defensive wing-half position he had mastered at Bury. In fact, so displeased was he with the status quo that when the manager expressed his intention to persist with the arrangement the following season, the normally calm and collected Lindsay involved himself in a blazing row with his boss that ended with the player handing in a transfer request. The board agreed to his demand and with plenty of other top clubs showing an interest his Anfield career looked unlikely to be extended beyond the seven appearances of his first term. At that moment, early in the 1970-71 campaign, fate took a hand and gave the 22 year old a chance in what had become the

Reds' problem position of left-back ever since the retirement of Gerry Byrne. Lindsay's performance against Newcastle that day was the most impressive seen there since the loss of Byrne and made it impossible to drop him from the role.

Bill Shankly was rarely one to publicise his mistakes, but the 200-odd games that his new left-back went on to play in that slot were a clear admission that the views of the owner of the 'mashie niblick' on its most effective range were for once rather more accurate than those of the expert watching from the gallery.

Struggling at the top

The youngster's failure to speak out sooner over his discomfort as a striker was probably due to what he later revealed as his awestruck difficulty in adjusting to life at such a high-profile club, but by the end of his first season of more regular football he had played in an FA Cup final and was sufficiently settled to be beginning to show the form that would make him arguably the finest – and certainly the most underrated – of left-backs in England.

Away from football, Alec enjoyed outdoor sports and the quiet of the countryside, to such an extent that as a young pro he and his brother actually kept pigs at their family home, yet on the field his style was anything but agricultural. A tough enough tackler to spark memories of Gerry Byrne, he was a far

Lindsay was one of Liverpool's most constructive defenders when he had the ball at his feet and would regularly move forward down the flank to link up with his attackers and fire in dangerous crosses from the left.

more complete player than his predecessor, particularly in his use of the ball, and formed two especially productive partnerships during the remainder of his Liverpool career. Lindsay was uniformly accurate throughout his entire range of passing and made a regular habit of picking out Kevin Keegan with perfectly weighted and directed passes through the inside-left channel. When he was not doing that, the tall defender liked to draw on his midfielder's past by carrying the ball down the wing before linking up with Steve Heighway to play a one-two that would give him the space to swing in one of the pin-point centres for which his left boot was also rightly famed. On the downside, Alec was never the quickest of players and he lacked as much confidence in his right foot as he had faith in its partner, to the extent that he would often shun chances to cross instantly with that peg in order to manoeuvre the ball onto his favoured side. But with a left foot as cultured as Alec Lindsay's, that was a small criticism indeed for he did more damage en route to the 1972-73 double of League and UEFA Cup with one weapon than most players could with two.

As his prolific season in the reserves suggested, his attacking expertise extended into areas other than just his passing, and his surprisingly low goals total does not reflect the explosiveness of his shot, which was especially effective from free-kicks and penalties. After settling in at left-back, Lindsay found himself inside the opposition's penalty area in open play far less often than in his initial brief spell in attack. One of the most profitable occasions on which he did pop up in the danger zone came in the first leg of the 1972-73 UEFA Cup semi-final against Tottenham Hotspur. His goal gave the Reds a 1-0 lead to take to London and meant that the away goal Steve Heighway grabbed in the subsequent 2-1 defeat at White Hart Lane was enough to send the Anfield side through to the final.

Back in the capital just a year later, Lindsay provided the nation with the finest possible example of his finishing prowess when he scored what would have been the best goal of the 1974 FA Cup final had his effort not been ruled out for offside, but it is some consolation that the 'goal' is as well remembered among Liverpool fans as the three legitimate strikes that saw off Newcastle United at Wembley.

International recognition

The full-back's career looked set to really take off after that success, as he followed it up by finally breaking into the international set-up. Despite winning England youth honours while at Bury, Alec had been consistently overlooked by Alf Ramsey, and it took the World Cup winner's replacement by caretaker-boss Joe Mercer for him to be given his chance.

That spell of success appeared at the time to herald the advent of a golden era for the strong defender, but it was to be, instead, the final glory of his career. Lindsay ran into a trough of poor form during 1975 that was compounded in October that year by an injury suffered in a UEFA Cup match against Real Sociedad in San Sebastian. And on his return to fitness, he found that the form of first Phil Neal and then Joey Jones left him on the fringes of the action, and he never played for the club at senior level again, moving on to Stoke City in September 1977 after two years of fruitless struggle to re-establish himself in the side. It is in the memory rather than in the record books that the talents of Alec Lindsay live on among those of the true Anfield greats.

Career History
Born: Bury, 27 February 1948
Signed: March 1969, from Bury
Full debut: Liverpool 10 Dundalk 0, Fairs Cup first round, 16 September 1969
Games: 246 (two as sub)
Goals: 18

International Caps
Four England caps

Honours
UEFA Cup 1972-73; League Championship 1972-73; FA Cup 1973-74

Other Clubs
Bury, Stoke City, Oakland (USA)

Terry McDermott

When you are a triple European Cup winner, have become the first man to win both the PFA and football writers' Player of the Year awards in the same season and are your club's practical joker in chief, self-confidence is just about the last commodity you would expect to be lacking. Yet throughout his Anfield career Terry McDermott lived in constant fear for his place and always expected to be the first to be criticised when things went wrong. He never considered himself to be anything more than 'a bread and butter player' who had to make up in enthusiasm for what he lacked in skill, and even the double honour afforded him in 1980 by his playing peers and those who chronicle the game from the stands failed to convince him otherwise. Those judges, however, knew what they were talking about and while he was never the most complete footballer to wear the red shirt, McDermott's influence was sufficiently strong actually to change the way in which Liverpool played.

He was in and out of the team for much of the first two seasons that followed his

Terry McDermott in European Cup action against FC Zurich in 1977. The slim midfielder was one of the most natural athletes Anfield has seen – despite his existence on a diet of chip butties!

£160,000 move from Newcastle in 1974, but once he established himself in the side his surging runs down the flank enabled the side to develop a 4-4-2 formation after the

Like many of his team-mates, McDermott's finest hour came on the 1977 night that Liverpool lifted the European Cup for the first time. The Mönchengladbach defence can only watch as Terry opens the scoring.

previous three-man attack of Keegan, Toshack and Heighway had been broken up. That price-less ability to get up and down the line, switching from defence to attack and back again in an instant, was the most striking aspect of Terry's game. The enduring image of his time at Anfield is of the willowy midfielder striding forward, curly perm shimmering in his slipstream, either to take a pass on the run and thunder in a shot on goal or to arrive unstoppably in con-necting with a deep cross to the far post.

A good goal getter

His record of hitting the net about once every four games was by no means unimpressive for a wide midfielder playing in a team that garnered goals from almost every position. McDermott was never afraid to have a pop at the target: as a Kirkby schoolboy he once broke a crossbar with the sheer force of his shot. The goal with which he opened the scoring in the 1977 European Cup final after sweeping typically onto Steve Heighway's through ball was the one he rated as the best of his career, but many others stand out almost as highly, such as the far-post header with which he rounded off the scintillating move he had set in motion from almost beneath his own bar during the 7-0 thrashing of Ardiles and Villa's Tottenham Hotspur in 1978.

A hat-trick against Hamburg in the Super Cup marked a turning point in Terry's Liverpool career, as it gave him the confidence to keep on trying his luck in front of goal. His scoring rate continued to improve, and he struck almost 40 goals in the 100 league games during his final three seasons. Previously, he had lacked the self-belief to impose himself in the attacking third of the field, particularly during the lengthy learning period he had to go through on his arrival at Anfield. Another boyhood Reds fan, McDermott had been the only Newcastle player not reduced to tears by the Magpies' loss to Liverpool in the 1974 FA Cup final, but his homecoming just six months later gave him something of a rude awakening as he had to make some major changes to his game in order to slot into his new club's style of play.

Passing and pushing on

Bob Paisley reckoned that Terry used to have a 30-minute 'kip' in the middle of most matches, and apart from improving his concentration the manager had also to free him from the habit of standing back to admire the telling pass he had just played instead of pushing on in search of a return. The lithe midfielder was the most willing of pupils and quickly became a far better player. For all that, though, it was Terry's natural athleticism that remained his greatest strength. Quick off the mark, deceptively strong and with the stamina and flowing stride of a thoroughbred racehorse, he was also blessed with the ability to eat what he liked without putting weight on. He hadn't enjoyed the diet of raw eggs, cod liver oil and malt his first club Bury made his father feed him every night in an attempt to fill out the skinny 16-year-old's lightweight frame, but at Liverpool his appetite and eating habits passed into club legend, especially his penchant for the chip butties he would demand in even the most high class of hotels, being prepared to construct his own from french fries and a baguette if necessary.

His individual tastes were just one of the foibles that made him one of Anfield's real characters. McDermott always played and trained with a smile on his face and his comic antics meant that laughter was never far from his team-mates either. A man for his pint and a day at the races, Terry once caused chaos on a trip to Japan when he had countless victims vainly pursuing a five pound note he was trailing around on a piece of string, before swapping the Sterling for Yen and repeating the trick on the locals. However, he often felt that his laid-back, apparently almost casual approach to the game and his reputation as team jester counted against him on the pitch. In his final years at Anfield he was sometimes singled out as the target for the crowd's collective ire when the team was not performing to its expected standards. That feeling of mild persecution contributed to Terry's generally unjustified worries over the security of his place in the team.

He was never afraid to get stuck in and plough his furrow on the flank for the full 90 minutes of a match, but it was Terry McDermott's ball skills, passing ability and the intelligent running with which he opened up defences at will that contributed most to a Liverpool career that earned him 11 major medals during his eight impressive seasons at the club.

Career History

Born: Kirkby, 8 December 1951
Signed: November 1974, from Newcastle United
Full debut: Everton 0 Liverpool 0, Division One, 16 November 1974
Games: 322 (12 as sub)
Goals: 75

International Caps

25 England caps, three goals

Honours

European Cup 1976-77, 1977-78, 1980-81; UEFA Cup 1975-76; League Championship 1975-76, 1976-77, 1978-79, 1979-80, 1981-82; League Cup 1980-81, 1981-82

Other Clubs

Bury, Newcastle United

Steve McMahon

There are few great football teams that have not built their reputations on a fine blend of steel and skill; even fewer have been able to call upon such a potent mixture in a single player. Throughout the 1980s, Liverpool could count themselves among the latter category, for while Graeme Souness left for Italy four years into that decade, the quintessential ball-playing hard man was missed for little more than a year. The arrival of Steve McMahon saw to that.

The young McMahon had earned rave reviews in a modest Everton side at the start of the decade, and his failure to settle after a move to Aston Villa opened the door for Kenny Dalglish to bring the combative midfielder back to his native Merseyside in 1985. Ironically, Steve might have come to Anfield direct from Goodison two years earlier but the strength of reaction the proposed move stirred up within the Blue half of the city made him think twice. Now, with Liverpool having drawn their first trophy blank in a decade during their initial season post-Souness, both parties seized on the chance to resurrect the deal and for £375,000 the new manager made his first signing. He would make few shrewder ones. McMahon went on to become the driving force behind the Reds team that won five major trophies in as many years.

Souness was the most inimitable of players and his majestic midfield presence still cast a long shadow across the Anfield pitch when his replacement first stepped on to its surface in the colours of his new club. However, McMahon was both confident enough in his own abilities and sufficiently strong-minded to resist the temptation of trying to live up to the reputation of his powerful predecessor. Those who tried to match Souness during his years in England invariably focused all their energies on emulating the cold hardness that radiated from his uncompromisingly physical approach rather than the subtler nuances of his skilful, creative side, and McMahon had previously been among those to suffer by comparison, being sent off for skirmishing with the tough Scot at Anfield in 1983. Perhaps he learned from that experience, for when he eventually inherited his erstwhile protagonist's number 11 jersey at Liverpool he soon revealed himself as a force to be spoken of if not quite in exactly the same breath as Souness then in certainly the same conversation. It is no coincidence that discussions of the shortcomings of the Reds teams of the early 1990s tend to conclude that what they needed most was a ballwinner of the class of Souness or McMahon; for the latter player's exertions in that role put him head and shoulders above all similar Liverpool players bar one.

Keeping good company

Such regular mention of Souness' name is a compliment to McMahon rather than a knocking slight, as few other players are worthy of being considered in the same class and so many aspects of his game were reminiscent of the Reds' most successful captain at his very best. 'Macca', as the former Goodison ball-boy was obviously titled by the Kop, governed the centre of the park and tackled with a controlled and determined aggression that was instantly recognisable to the fans. He possessed plenty of craft and guile, but never displayed quite the same unsurpassable vision and exquisite range of passing that Souness offered his side, although McMahon's invariably accurate distribution did become even more perceptive as he grew in experience. His preference, however, was to keep things simple in midfield and keep the play moving forward, picking out his attackers with intelligent balls that created immediate danger for the opposition. Those skills were really brought to the fore by the arrival of John Barnes and Peter Beardsley at the start of the 1987-88 season, whose inviting presence saw Steve emerge as a playmaking talent equal to his stature as a ballwinner.

The highlight of Liverpool's greatest year

His creative side was never developed at the expense of his natural tenacity and determination, however, for it was those qualities that gave him the solid platform on which to express himself. And never did he demonstrate that combination in more emphatic fashion than when setting up the goal with which John Aldridge opened the scoring in the spectacular 2-0 defeat of Arsenal in January 1988.

A long spell of mounting Liverpool pressure had been matched by a similar welling up of anticipation on the heaving Kop, but as the first half entered its final minute with the visitors apparently having scrambled yet another attack towards the relative safety of a throw-in, it looked as though both players and spectators were to be denied the goal they craved. McMahon, however, had other ideas and set off in a headlong dash to prevent the ball from running out of play. He stopped it dead on the touchline and although his momentum took him charging into the front row of the stand he managed to extricate himself and reach the ball fractionally ahead of the nearest Arsenal defender. Fired up by his exertions, Macca tore past two opponents before slipping a perfect pass through the visitors' back line, allowing Peter Beardsley to whip a low cross across goal for Aldridge to slide into the net and trigger pandemonium on the Kop in salute to the most exhilarating goal of what was arguably Liverpool's most spectacular season.

McMahon actually took a little while to establish himself fully at Anfield and spent his first season battling with Kevin McDonald for a midfield berth. He played 23 games that Double-winning season, but after injuring himself during the FA Cup semi-final he could make only the

McMahon's reputation was as a midfield ballwinner, but over the years he added qualities of intelligent distribution and playmaking to the steel and determination that had first made his name.

bench at Wembley. Steve was only a steady scorer during his years with the Reds, but had a fierce and accurate right foot which he put to regular eye-catching use from distance. He quickly caught Ian Rush's habit of scoring prolifically against the club he supported as a boy, hitting his first Liverpool goal in a 3-2 win at Everton in September 1985, repeating the trick in the following season's 3-1 Goodison victory and scoring again in the very next league derby, this time at Anfield, which Liverpool took 2-0 in November 1987.

Most of his goals were piledrivers from around the edge of the penalty area, but the Littlewoods Cup hat-trick he struck against Leicester City in 1986-87 – the season in which he was voted the Reds' Player of the Year – demonstrated the full range of his finishing technique. Having struck five times in the previous round's 13-2 aggregate thrashing of Fulham, he now opened his account with a 30-yarder that flew in off the underside of the bar. He then carried the ball from inside his own half on a mazy dribble which ended with the cutest of curlers disguised perfectly by a sweetly executed dummy, and added his third by coolly side-stepping a desperate tackle inside the box and tapping home from close range. The following season, 1987-88, in which the solidity with which he anchored the midfield allowed Barnes and Beardsley to weave their magic ahead of him, Steve finally won a full England cap to go alongside the six Under-21 and two B-level honours he had already earned. However, he never really established himself in Bobby Robson's side, although his cause was not helped by tearing a tendon behind his knee by stretching over-enthusiastically for a ball he could not reach before a couple of important internationals in September 1988.

Losing speed

McMahon's passion cost him almost the entire second half of the 1990-91 season after he damaged knee ligaments while throwing himself into a rash challenge as the red mist descended during a fiercely fought Anfield derby. When he returned for the start of the following season the now 30-year-old McMahon seemed to have lost the edge off his pace. Liverpool's new manager Graeme Souness decided to sell Steve to Manchester City, for £900,000.

The price seemed a good one for a player that age and with his form at Maine Road never coming back to haunt the Reds, an acceptable piece of business appeared to have been done. But the true measure of McMahon's contribution to the Anfield cause lies in the fact that the gap in the side that his departure left was almost as big as the one created by Souness' farewell a decade earlier – and one that took even longer to fill.

Career History

Born: Liverpool, 20 August 1961
Signed: September 1985, from Aston Villa
Full debut: Oxford United 2 Liverpool 2, Division One, 14 September 1985
Games: 267 (two as sub)
Goals: 49

International Caps

17 England caps

Honours

League Championship 1985-86, 1987-88, 1989-90; FA Cup 1988-89

Other Clubs

Everton, Aston Villa, Manchester City, Swindon Town

Steve McManaman

While the appointment of Roy Evans to the Liverpool managership in 1994 was widely seen as heralding a return to the boot-room traditions of Shankly and Paisley, the team of individual talents he set about creating bore a stronger resemblance to the flair-packed late-1980s sides of Kenny Dalglish than to the efficient Red machines of the 1960s and 1970s. The freest spirit in that attack-minded line-up is Steve McManaman, the tousle-haired Scouser of the twiglet physique and dazzling feet. With a full England cap, winners' medals from FA Cup and League Cup finals and Man of the Match awards from both those games by the age of 23, McManaman's talent has always been a precocious one. As a small, skinny schoolboy he represented his city against teams a full year older than him; as a tall, skinny Anfield reserve he made his first appearances for the England Under-21 side against opponents up to three years older than him. And an eye-catching senior club debut against Oldham Athletic on the opening day of the following season prompted John Barnes to single the youngster out as an England star of the future. McManaman, who cleaned Barnes' boots as an apprentice, played as an out-and-out winger that day but it was his later success in the floating free role he was handed on Evans' accession that really catapulted him to the international recognition his senior team-mate had predicted for him.

By the time he graduated to the national team, winning his first cap as a substitute against Nigeria in November 1994, the only real surprise was that he had not been invited to do so sooner. Steve had stood out at every level at which he had played.

The rapid pace of his progress has been assured by a list of enviable attributes as long as one of his gangly legs, but his mental attitude and temperament have been just as important as his more obvious skills in establishing him as one of the very best in his business. Of the hundreds of professionals who have passed through the care of the Liverpool coaching staff, none has ever been more relaxed about their work than the almost horizontally laid-back McManaman. Although he has the standard trappings of footballing celebrity – the expensive car and

Steve McManaman has emerged as the most potent attacking force in Roy Evans' Liverpool team since being handed the free role in the side that has provided the perfect platform to show off his dribbling skills.

designer clothes – his priceless feet remain firmly on the ground and his head is still unturned by fame. As much as his enormous natural talent, that even temperament and his unusual level-headedness for one so

The laid back McManaman has never been overawed by the big occasion as two Man of the Match awards from his first two Wembley finals readily attest. Here he goes past Bolton's Richard Sneekes in the 1995 Coca Cola Cup final.

young give him the best chance of securing a more permanent place in footballing memory than has often been the lot of similarly gifted individualists.

Displaying brilliant skills

For unlike many more mercurial performers, McManaman's brilliance is a consistent and relentless one. A top-class distance runner who beat Olympic track star Curtis Robb as a kid, his stamina and concentration make him as potent a threat in the last minute of a match as in the first, and his level of performance rarely dips throughout the long arduous season. In the manner of almost every youngster who excels in his debut season, the articulate, unaffected lad from Walton faded a little the following term as the strain of 90 matches in two campaigns took its inevitable physical toll and he lost the advantage of surprise he had enjoyed as a Division One unknown; but the lessons of that learning experience have seen him develop into an ever more complete performer with each year that passes.

Defensive duties are not part of his brief, and as a roving attacker given the freedom to pop up wherever he feels he can cause the most damage McManaman is without peer in this country. With the ball at his feet and room to run in, Steve is at his best, slaloming his way past despairing tackles with a dip of the shoulder, a swaying step-over and an extra unexpected injection of pace to take him into the space he needs to feed his forwards. McManaman has never classed himself as an orthodox winger continually crossing from the bye-line and prefers to do his damage attacking the penalty area through the inside left and right channels. That approach regularly takes him into shooting range, and for someone who has played up front for the reserves and likes to curl accurate shots into the corner of the goal from around the edge of the box, his record of finding the net is disappointing. When he reacted to a fine FA Cup brace against Leeds United in 1996 by quipping that he had had so many chances that the law of averages said that two of them had to go in, he wasn't really joking. He reached double figures in both 1995-96 and 1996-97 — an acceptable return from a creative midfielder – but with a surer sense of direction he could have doubled those annual hauls.

McManaman's true forte is as the top flight's most precise deliverer of a pass and its undisputed master of finding the space to open up defences at will. His progress was hastened by the greater physical strength maturity has recently given him. In his earliest days, the pale, frail-looking urchin figure who claimed to get sunburned under floodlights could be muscled off the ball by older, tougher opponents. In recent seasons he has become capable of holding the ball up under pressure of increasingly popular man-marking, as much through his own strength as through his ball skills. Yet it is that fancy footwork which remains his and Liverpool's most deadly weapon. When McManaman plays well, so do Liverpool. On the rare occasions that he is off-colour, so is the whole team. It is no coincidence that the Reds' championship challenge fell away in the later stages of the 1996-97 season when the inevitable effects of almost three years of continuous football looked to be catching up on McManaman, who seemed in desperate need of the break that was finally afforded him by a summer knee operation.

Despite his fatigue, he still managed to score a crucial goal as a stand-in striker at Sunderland to keep Anfield's flickering title hopes alive for a week or two longer and reinforce his reputation as a man for the big occasion. In 1992 he had ended his first season by running the same opposition ragged at Wembley to help the Reds win the FA Cup. Three years later he returned to the twin towers to take another man of the match award, courtesy of the two spectacular individual goals that sealed League Cup final victory over Bolton Wanderers. Domestic football's biggest prize continues to elude him, however, although with a fit and fresh McManaman in their ranks it is inconceivable that Liverpool will not have many more chances to put that right.

Career History

Born: Liverpool, 11 February 1972
Signed: February 1990
Full debut: Liverpool 2 Oldham Athletic 1, Division One, 17 August 1991
Games: 283 (ten as sub)
Goals: 47

International Caps

18 England caps

Honours

FA Cup 1991-92; League Cup 1994-95

Jan Molby

Liverpool Football Club can have had few more talented servants in its entire existence than Jan Molby. Yet at the same time, if medals were ever handed out for unfulfilled potential then the big Dane would also be standing on top of the podium. Anfield thrilled to his breathtaking ball skills and laser-guided passing for more than a decade, but on far fewer occasions than it would have wished, for Molby's brilliance was tempered by a susceptibility to both injury and weight problems that limited his appearances in the first-team.

Joe Fagan made him Liverpool's first European import in the summer of 1984 as a 21-year-old replacement for Graeme Souness, who had moved to Italy. Adjusting to a foreign country was no problem for the 6ft 1in midfielder, as he had left his native Denmark at the age of just 18 to join Ajax, where he reportedly picked up an Amsterdam accent as strong as the Liverpudlian one with which he now delivers his English. Replacing the Reds' all-action leader was a somewhat taller order, however.

Caught in a speed trap

Three years learning his trade in Holland under the tutelage of the great Johan Cruyff ensured that Jan had all the necessary skill – in fact he was an even better ball player than Souness – but he failed to make an instant impact in the eye of the English game's hurricane pace. Unable to snipe at his ability, the critics drew a bead on his lack of speed and the size of his waistline. They had a point – although Molby's barrel-chested build, tree-trunk thighs and relatively small feet often made him look portlier than he actually was – and those were the two main factors behind his replacement by the grafting Kevin McDonald midway through that first season. A brief spell as sweeper towards the end of the term gave him more time and space in which to exhibit his vast array of passing skills, but it was back at the heart of the midfield action that he really made his mark in the next campaign.

Jan had lost several pounds over the summer – his fighting weight was 14st 7lb – and that advance, once allied to a greater

Jan Molby was plagued by injury and weight problems throughout the 12 years he spent at Liverpool, but when fit and in form the big Dane was arguably the most skilful player that Anfield has ever seen.

appreciation of the unique demands of our domestic game, brought massive dividends as Liverpool swept to the Double. He used his acute footballing brain and mesmeric

Molby bursts out of a tackle by Everton's Paul Bracewell during the 1986 FA Cup final. In a performance that was probably his most important in the red jersey, Molby set up two goals to help Liverpool clinch the Double.

close control to negate the need to perform at the breakneck pace of so many other lesser talents. While the action blurred around him, Molby exhibited the mark of true footballing class in always appearing to have time on the ball. An almost imperceptible shimmy was enough to send opponents lunging foolishly at fresh air, while he had such certainty in his own ability that he could look up in search of the next defence-splitting pass before he had finished stepping calmly out of a tackle. Never allowing himself to be hurried, he knew exactly when to put his foot on the ball, have a quick look up and switch the focus of attack from one flank to the unguarded space on the other.

A sizeable and positive force

Jan was always more of a creative force than a destructive one, but his size and strength made him a formidable tackler when the mood took him. He was also adept at putting that same weight behind his shots and was lethal from dead-ball situations. An unstoppably powerful and unerringly accurate penalty taker – he scored a hat-trick from the spot against Coventry City in 1986 – he was also a free-kick specialist who could combine brute force with spectacular bend. Those attributes helped him to the runners-up spot in the Anfield scoring charts that Double year, and none of the goals he scored was more important than the penalty he converted at Watford with just four minutes standing between Liverpool and an FA Cup exit at the quarter-final stage. As his team-mates shied away from the responsibility, Molby remained the coolest man in the ground, striking the ball with not a hint of nerves to set up the extra-time finale in which Ian Rush slotted home the winner. But Jan saved his finest display of that season for the FA Cup final itself. With Liverpool trailing 1-0 to Everton, Molby stood up to be counted, playing a perfect through-ball for Rush to level the scores, and repeating the dose to allow the Welshman to set up Craig Johnston for the second goal of an eventual 3-1 win.

What should have been the platform for the Dane to go on and establish himself as Liverpool's finest midfielder became the pinnacle of his Anfield career. The following term he played well in what was by Liverpool's standards a mediocre campaign, the high point coming when he set up Ian Rush's goal in the Littlewoods Cup final defeat by Arsenal. But a broken foot suffered in training restricted him to just seven league outings with the record-breaking 1987-88 side, and ultimately proved to be a setback from which he never really recovered. That problem seemed to plunge him into a vicious circle of injury, in which he put on weight while unable to train and then found that his subsequent state of unfitness on returning to action put him at risk of suffering further harm, thereby triggering the whole process again.

Crime and punishment

Frustrated by continuing inactivity, Jan added to his troubles with a string of high-profile off-field incidents that led at least one newspaper cuttings library to open two files on him – one titled 'footballing stories', the other 'non-footballing stories' – and culminated in him serving a three-month jail term for motoring offences during the 1988-89 season. The club showed admirable loyalty to Molby in standing by him, and he repaid their faith by emerging from custody in the best physical shape of his Anfield life and with a determination to win back his place in the side. He did just that, and then began the following season with as fine a series of displays as had ever been seen from him. However, after a run of games that only just sneaked into double figures, injury struck again and this time he failed to bounce back with the resilience that he had displayed in the past. Although he played in the 1992 FA Cup final against Sunderland, he featured only in fits and starts during his last six seasons before taking up the offer of a player-manager's job at Swansea City in February 1996.

The big man from Jutland never lost his silken skills and instinctive artistry throughout those final years and the fans always loved to see him on song. And not just those at Anfield either, for his mere presence in the Barnsley side to which he was loaned during his final term with the Reds was enough to draw an extra 3,000 people through the Oakwell gates. Jan Molby gave even greater pleasure to thousands more Liverpool fans in his 12 years at the club, but he frustrated them just as much through his failure to make the long-term impression his talent truly deserved.

Career History
Born: Kolding, Denmark, 4 July 1963
Signed: August 1984, from Ajax Amsterdam
Full debut: Norwich 3 Liverpool 3, Division One, 25 August 1984
Games: 280 (30 as sub)
Goals: 58

International Caps
25 Denmark caps

Honours
League Championship 1985-86, 1989-90; FA Cup 1985-86, 1991-92

Other Clubs
Kolding IF, Ajax Amsterdam, Swansea City

Phil Neal

When Chris Lawler's career was effectively ended by injury in November 1973, many Reds fans must have wondered if the club would ever see a right-back of his quality and consistency again. The wait for a worthy successor lasted just one year, not the lifetime that most observers had expected, for once Phil Neal took his place in the Liverpool line-up he made himself such a permanent fixture that the records of reliability he set may never be equalled. Neal missed just one league game in his first ten years at the club and after a dead leg forced him out of a European Cup trip to Trabzonspor in October 1976 he embarked on an incredible run of 417 consecutive appearances for the Reds. He would go on to surpass Lawler's previous milestone by just over 100 matches and before injury finally caught up with him in 1983 he was beginning to look almost indestructible.

Phil Neal was a worthy heir to the attacking right-back legacy of Chris Lawler and proved himself even more consistent than his predecessor. He missed just one game in ten years and put together a run of 417 consecutive appearances.

Playing for the jersey

His amazing ability to keep on keeping on stemmed more from an almost feverish determination not to relinquish his hold on the jersey than from any particular luck with injuries. Neal suffered his fair share of bumps and bruises but was always prepared to play through the pain barrier. He once dangerously defied doctor's orders to turn out in a league game just three days after undergoing surgery on a depressed cheek-bone, and on another occasion played for eight weeks with his usual size seven boot on one foot and an eight and a half on the other to accommodate the makeshift plaster cast he had made Ronnie Moran fit to a painful broken toe.

Phil was particularly proud of his record of first-team service and the fact that he only ever played six reserve games for the club. Even when achilles trouble forced him to miss a pre-season tour, such was his need to get back into action that he insisted on flying out to join the side 10 days later. He always put his achievement down to the same 'nosey' inquisitiveness which had earlier ensured he never missed a single day's school, but there was more to it than that. For after six years at Northampton Town, Phil Neal was desperate to play First Division football and when his chance came in October 1974 he was determined to savour every second of the experience and never take any of it for granted lest he found himself swiftly returned from whence he came. That was unsurprising given the unedifying surroundings of the Fourth Division in which he was practising his art – at a club where pay cheques were handed out on Fridays with the express instructions that they were not to be cashed until the following Wednesday – and the length of time he had spent there. When Bob Paisley weighed in with the modest £60,000 bid that took him to Anfield, Neal must have been beginning to wonder whether the call would ever come.

Paisley saw Neal as a utility player who could figure throughout the defence, and as the new man had spent the last two-thirds of the game in goal when chief scout Geoff Twentyman had been to watch him, that wasn't too far off the mark. In fact, it was as a left-back that Phil made his Liverpool debut when the manager threw him into the cauldron of a Goodison derby just a month after his arrival. Although having settled on his inclusion by Friday afternoon, Paisley sent the 23 year old home under the impression he was playing for the reserves the next day so that he would enjoy a sound night's sleep unhindered by nerves. Called up in the morning, Neal walked from Anfield to Goodison with all the fans, clutching his boots in a brown paper bag. If no one knew who he was before kick-off, his performance in the goalless draw that followed, and in alternating between the two full-back berths for the next season, soon made his face among the best known in the city. Over the next 11 years, Neal would win 16 major trophies and tot up the half century of international appearances that made him England's most capped right-back.

Making the right moves

The fitness and reliability that enabled him to build such a record were among the most obvious of his footballing virtues, but in his ball skills, positional play and attacking flair he was also a worthy successor to Chris Lawler. Successive managers encouraged him to push forward as often as possible to see the moves he began through to their completion, and the intuitive understanding he built up through the years with Jimmy Case, Terry McDermott and Sammy Lee made his excursions into enemy territory particularly profitable. He had a knack similar to Lawler's of arriving in the penalty box at precisely the moment of maximum opportunity, yet although he scored only one goal fewer than his predecessor, and at only a marginally slower rate, many of Phil's goals came from the penalty spot. He had been the regular taker at Northampton, and took over the duties at Anfield after Kevin Keegan fluffed a couple during the first half of the 1975-76 season. His first two penalties came in the same match, against Arsenal in the December of that campaign, and were both tucked away with the confidence for which he soon became famous in such situations.

Neal missed only four of the first 24 penalties he took over the next two and a half years, but a couple of failures caused him to hand the responsibility over to Terry McDermott towards the end of 1978. By then he had of course scored the most famous of all his penalties, to put Liverpool out of sight against Borussia Mönchengladbach in the 1977 European Cup final, and by the time he was next required to step up to the spot in the continent's most important

match, he was once again the Reds' regular expert. On the same ground, but at the opposite end to his original effort, Phil buried his penalty in the 1984 shoot-out against Roma with customary decisiveness.

Phil Neal is the only man to appear in all five of Liverpool's European Cup finals and is the only player to score in more than one of them. Here he shows off the trophy after the defeat of Roma in their own Olympic Stadium in 1984.

Before that drama, however, Neal had actually handed Liverpool a lead in open play when he stabbed the ball home from close range. That goal revealed how even after a full decade's service to the club he was still being encouraged to push on into the opponents' box to follow his attacks through, and his determination to do just that meant he had lingered long enough up front to be in the right spot at the right time to strike. His attacking style was effective but unfussy, built around perceptive distribution, either through the inside right channel or pulled across from the goal-line, and intelligent overlaps fed by one-twos performed with his mid-fielders. And so cultured was the constructive side of his game that in 1978 Italian legend Gianni Rivera named him in his fantasy World XI alongside such luminaries as Zico, Roberto Rivelino and Johan Cruyff.

Phil's defending was equally graceful and his approach was far more cerebral than physical, using his fine positional sense to shepherd and jockey wingers into the areas of least danger rather than railroad them into touch with a thumping tackle. He wasn't the quickest of full-backs and preferred to do his defending as far forward as possible, where any free-kicks he was forced to concede when found wanting for pace were unlikely to set the alarm bells ringing. A self-confessed 'giggler' and the only man to appear in all five of Liverpool's European Cup finals, his experience and talkative nature made him an obvious choice as captain when Graeme Souness left for Sampdoria in 1984. His leadership was only brief, however, because Steve Nicol was soon putting his place under ever increasing pressure that, at the age of 34, he found impossible to resist.

By 1985 Phil was beginning to contemplate a move into management, but the fact that he eventually did so with Bolton rather than Liverpool heralded a brief falling out with his former colleagues at Anfield. Neal's belief that he was a clear favourite to succeed Joe Fagan after Heysel left him severely piqued by the subsequent appointment of Kenny Dalglish and some ill-advised comments in the right-back's autobiography a year later saw his erstwhile team-mate serve him with a High Court writ. That brief and quickly forgotten episode should not be allowed to cloud an Anfield career that was as rich in memories as it was in prizes, for no other Red has won as many trophies with the club as Neal did during his time at Anfield, and Phil himself would certainly never want to find himself estranged from the institution for whom he laboured so tirelessly for so long.

Happy days

His years at Liverpool had provided him with more good memories than any player could ever dare to expect from the game and in a gesture of thanks to the club and the people of the city for giving him the happiest days of his professional life he loaned his entire medal collection to the Reds' museum. For 11 years of unprece- dented success, the Anfield public owes Phil Neal just as big a debt of gratitude.

Career History

Born: Irchester, Northants, 29 February 1951
Signed: October 1974, from Northampton Town
Full debut: Everton 0 Liverpool 0,
Division One, 16 November 1974
Games: 635 (two as sub)
Goals: 60

International Caps

50 England caps, five goals

Honours

European Cup 1976-77, 1977-78, 1980-81, 1983-84; UEFA Cup 1975-76; League Championship 1975-76, 1976-77, 1978-79, 1979-80, 1981-82, 1982-83, 1983-84; League Cup 1980-81, 1981-82, 1982-83, 1983-84

Other Clubs

Northampton Town, Bolton Wanderers

Steve Nicol

In his 13 years as a Liverpool player, Steve Nicol covered literally every blade of grass on the Anfield pitch in pursuit of glory with the Reds. As his team's most adaptable utility player he appeared in every outfield position at one time or another. Such versatility had already been hinted at before Nicol was snapped up by Bob Paisley in 1981, as the former Ayr United right-back had appeared for Scotland Under-21s on both sides of the defence in a string of performances that were convincing enough to persuade Liverpool to shell out £300,000 for his services. That was a not inconsiderable fee to pay for a 19 year old, but the player himself was under no illusions that it guaranteed him an instant passport to the first team. With the ever reliable Phil Neal still going as strong as ever, that was just as well. And when Nicol did get a brief taste of league action in his second season south of the border, it was in midfield rather than in defence, standing in for Ronnie Whelan twice and replacing Craig Johnston on a further two occasions.

Lucky numbers

The next campaign, however, saw him make a more permanent breakthrough as Liverpool landed a unique Treble of League, European Cup and Milk Cup. This time he appeared in the number two, five, 11 and 12 shirts – and impressed in every one of them. A solid tackler who read the play well and covered the ground quickly in his size 14 boots, Nicol was a confident stand-in for Neal early on in the season, displaying a similar willingness to press forward down the flank, before playing the remainder of his 38 matches in midfield. In fact, Steve looked such a find on the right wing – where he played for much of the following term – that even after he had reverted to right-back following Neal's departure in the first-half of the 1985-86 Double-winning season, Bob Paisley was still singing his praises as a winger. And with good reason too: Nicol was as comfortable going forward as he was in defence. A dominant presence in the air at a relatively small 5ft 10in, it was with the ball at his giant feet that he really excelled. By matching the calmness of Alan Hansen he was able to squeeze into the great centre-half's considerably smaller shoes for a short spell in the late 1980s and showed that he was equally at ease delivering a pinpoint pass out from the back or dribbling clear of trouble himself. That skill on the ball was also put to regular deadly effect in the opposition's rear third of the field, where Steve always gave his team another attacking option, particularly in his raids down the flanks.

Steve Nicol rarely received the acclaim given to some of his colleagues in the great Liverpool sides of the 1980s. But his all-round ability and positional play earned him real respect among his fellow professionals.

Nicol holds the League Championship trophy aloft at Anfield. He won the league four times and was voted Footballer of the Year in 1989 – ironically one of the few occasions when Liverpool missed out on the title.

Possessing the confidence to take defenders on on either side, once past them he had the ability to cross accurately with both feet, as well as knowing where the goal was himself. Despite that eye for an opening, it was only in emergencies that he was occasionally thrown forward as a striker and he managed less than one goal for every ten games that he played. But his first Anfield goal was one to savour; a diving near-post header to round off a 3-0 win over Everton in November 1983. And savoured it was, admitted Nicol later, with a weekend that was 'drowned in a sea of alcohol!'

He knocked in a further six goals that season, but as the campaign reached its climax with the glamour of the European Cup final in Rome he would briefly have swapped all those strikes and more to erase just one potentially decisive miss. Having entered the match against Roma as a late substitute he forced a fine save out of the Italian goalkeeper Franco Tancredi with his first touch before the tie went to penalties. No order for taking the spot kicks had been officially agreed among the Liverpool players and management in advance, but before any impromptu rota could be drawn up Nicol grabbed the ball and, perhaps impetuously, stepped up to take the first kick. He skied his effort, but before the full potential implications of his miss had sunk in his team-mates had redeemed the situation and the Scot was collecting club football's greatest prize at the age of just 22.

A successful Scots colony

The youngster's willingness to take that nerve-jangling first penalty may have been an expression of his confidence in his own ability to match the efforts of football's finest when the stakes were highest, but off the field he was never quite so worldly wise. On his first day at Anfield he found himself changing between his heroes Kenny Dalglish and Alan Hansen, and soon fell in with the Scottish contingent whose other leader was Graeme Souness. As the junior partner in the firm, the trusting Nicol soon found himself not only the others' 'gofer' but also the butt of their practical jokes. He was once abandoned on the freezing hard shoulder of the M6 after the others, all heading for an international in Glasgow, had persuaded him to retrieve a jumper from the car boot, but he had an answer of his own to a far more elaborate hoax in the run-up to that 1984 European Cup final. Convinced by his team-mates that Dalglish's reluctance to stay for a drink in the bar was because he had recently been diagnosed as terminally ill he approached Kenny – who was in on the gag – for confirmation. Told that this was indeed the case, he replied: 'Oh, I wondered why you'd been playing so badly.'

But the ribbing was never anything less than affectionate because his colleagues knew better than anyone the Scottish international's worth. His ability and willingness to play wherever he was needed had left him somewhat neglected in the wider public eye by dint of his not being instantly identifiable with one particular position. Broader recognition of his talent came eventually from within his profession at large in 1989, when he became one of only a small number of defenders to be voted the PFA's Footballer of the Year. Nicol himself reckoned that he had been in finer form during the previous term, when Liverpool stormed to the title on the back of a record-equalling 29-match unbeaten run that stretched from the beginning of the season to the following March.

Plucky strikes

Playing then at left-back, Steve's willingness to link up with new boy John Barnes saw him begin the campaign in as explosive a manner as the team itself. A winning goal at Highbury on opening day was followed up with two more in a 4-1 win at Coventry. A League Cup strike at Blackburn arrived during late September, but sandwiched in between was a spectacular televised hat-trick at Newcastle, scored this time after he had switched to the right of midfield. Steve actually had a fourth goal disallowed in that game, but the match-ball clincher was the one that stood out for him as the best goal of his career – a neat chip over the advancing goalkeeper after taking play on from near the halfway line. That unheralded record of seven goals in as many games equalled Nicol's totals for 1983-84 and 1984-85 and gave his team-mates a new joke for the dressing room. And no doubt his failure to net again in the remaining 43 games of the season gave them yet another!

Steve Nicol left Anfield early in 1995 to take up a player-coach's position at Notts County, but less than a year later he found himself back in the Premiership shoring up the Sheffield Wednesday defence and looking as though he had never been away. Without his steadying presence for the latter part of that season, the Owls might not have avoided the drop. And quite simply, without his composure, skill and versatility over more than a decade, Liverpool might not have accumulated the astonishing array of silverware that they did in Steve Nicol's time at the club.

Career History

Signed: October 1981, from Ayr United
Full debut: Birmingham City 0 Liverpool 0, Division One, 31 August 1982
Games: 453 (16 as sub)
Goals: 43

International Caps

27 Scotland caps

Honours

European Cup 1983-84; League Championship 1983-84, 1985-86, 1987-88, 1989-90; FA Cup 1985-86, 1988-89

Other Clubs

Ayr United, Notts County, Sheffield Wednesday

Bob Paisley

That Bob Paisley had what it took to become the most successful manager in the history of English football was obvious long before he succeeded Bill Shankly in the summer of 1974. All the teams that he sent out to conquer England and Europe in the late 1970s and early 1980s were blessed with the qualities of skill, steel, intelligence and a refusal to admit defeat that he had displayed himself in the red jersey a full 30 years earlier. While at the Anfield helm, the shy former bricklayer always shunned the limelight and was uncomfortable with praise of his own astonishing achievements, happier when talk switched to the work of Bill Shankly in laying the foundations of the Anfield dynasty, even if the conversation did overlook his own enormous contribution to that task. Shankly's larger than life persona overshadowed his less quotable successor's reign, but in turn the scale of Paisley's accomplishments as a manager have meant his exploits as a player are rarely remembered. That is a shame, for the tough North Easterner was as important to Liverpool's first postwar successes on the field as he was off it in later years.

Bob Paisley arrived at Anfield as an FA Amateur Cup winner, but never managed to lift the professional equivalent as either a player or manager, although he was involved in Cup successes as a coach.

Tricky treats

Bob's playing days yielded just a single League Championship medal to set against the 19 major titles he won in nine years as Anfield boss, but like many similarly gifted stars of his generation, he lost six prime years of his career to World War II. Signed in 1939 as an FA Amateur Cup winner from Bishop Auckland, Paisley wasted little time in becoming a favourite of the Anfield crowd. The Kop loved his tough tackling and the tricks of skill he would cheekily trot out from time to time. Regulars of that era still recall the sight of the wing-half running down the wing with the ball balanced on the top of his head or bouncing a quick throw-in off the back of a retreating, unsuspecting opponent to enable him to play on himself!

But that was just about the extent of his flamboyance. When it came to the serious business of defending there were few opponents who relished coming up against his no-nonsense approach. His iron tackling was the most valuable facet of his game and

Paisley was a skilful wing-half in his playing days, but it was the steel with which he played that was his greatest contribution to Liverpool's success in the first post-war League Championship of 1946-47.

his appetite for the fray was so voracious that a Liverpool *Daily Post* match report of 1947 went as far as declaring him 'the toughest man of 51,911 people' inside Anfield.

Although Paisley scored only 13 goals in the 278 games he played for Liverpool before joining the backroom staff in 1954, he saved at least one of his strikes for the most important of occasions. The lost war years of the 1946-47 champions meant they peaked with that title triumph and soon found themselves beginning to decline with age. But three years later they still had an FA Cup run left in them and progressed to a Maine Road semi-final meeting with Everton. An injury to Laurie Hughes saw Bill Jones – grandfather of Rob – bring Bob Paisley into the side. He gave the Reds a crucial first-half lead with a perfectly judged lob, to which Billy Liddell added a second after the break. Hughes recovered for the final against Arsenal, but it was Paisley rather than Jones who was asked to step down for the big day. Liverpool lost 2-0 at Wembley and many of his team-mates and an even greater proportion of the fans believed that events would have unfolded in an altogether different manner had the miner's son from County Durham been included. Bob always looked back on that as the lowest moment of his career. He had the wit to turn that disappointment to his own eventual benefit; in later life he was able to tell a player genuinely that he knew how he felt when breaking the news that he would be the odd man out for a big game.

Thinking in the bath

Paisley's experiences as a player stood him in good stead when he moved into coaching and management. He had already shown a thoughtful approach to the game while still playing. While most players were happy simply to have won, regardless of manner, and even keener to forget about a match they had just lost, Bob would go over the key moments of each game in the bath afterwards, discussing the factors that had contributed to a victory or running through the goals that had cost his side the points and working out how the mistakes that led to them could be avoided in future. That was Paisley the thinker, exercising the brain that would work out the fine details of Bill Shankly's master plan and later create some of the most tactically astute football teams the European game has seen.

There was also Bob Paisley the fighter, driven by the indomitable spirit that he later instilled into his sides. Team-mate Albert Stubbins recalls one hard-fought defeat by Everton in which Paisley's all-action performance left him so drained and spent that at the final whistle he was incapable of walking up the stairs to the Goodison dressing rooms, and had to haul himself agonisingly up the hand rail, a step at a time. 'If he had that sort of mentality as a player,' said Stubbins, 'I'm not surprised that those Liverpool teams he managed were so full of fighting spirit and effort: Bob wouldn't have tolerated a team that didn't give every single ounce it had.'

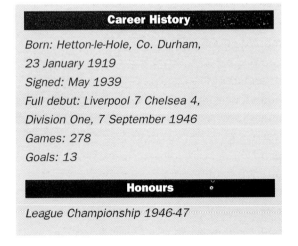

Career History

Born: Hetton-le-Hole, Co. Durham,
23 January 1919
Signed: May 1939
Full debut: Liverpool 7 Chelsea 4,
Division One, 7 September 1946
Games: 278
Goals: 13

Honours

League Championship 1946-47

Jamie Redknapp

Not many seven year olds are thrown out of an Under-11s league for being too good, but then Jamie Redknapp has always been one of the game's early learners. He was never among the gangs of schoolchildren who hang around football clubs' training grounds straining for a glimpse of their heroes. Rather than watch his local team go through their paces on the practice pitch he was out there with them. He made his debut for Bournemouth – then managed by his father Harry – at the tender age of 16 and impressed quickly enough for Kenny Dalglish to shell out £350,000 for him after just 13 games, in 1991. Just over a year later he became the youngest player to represent Liverpool in Europe when Graeme Souness gave him a debut at Auxerre in the UEFA Cup.

A class act

Redknapp's class impressed immediately but three seasons of internal Anfield strife did not help him settle into the central midfield role that is both the most pivotal and toughest to master on the entire pitch, and it was only when stability swept back with the old broom of Roy Evans that his development began to gather real momentum. Growing up in a footballing family gave Jamie a rare confidence and level-headedness that has stood him in good stead for coping as much with the thousand teeny crushes that trail almost every footballer who can open a jar of hair gel as with the less affectionate attentions of the Premiership's midfielders. His easy, stylish skill on the ball was of more help in avoiding the latter trouble, but during his first three terms, in which he

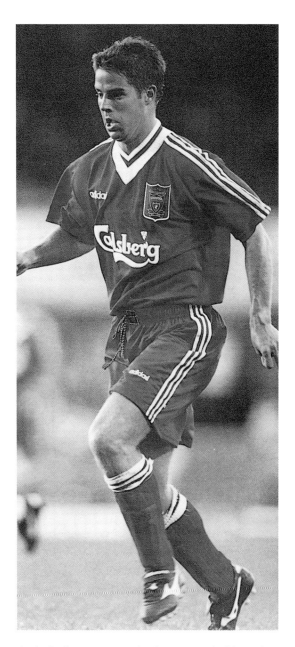

Jamie Redknapp appeared to be set to make his mark on the 1995-96 season at both club and international level when a serious hamstring injury suffered in the opening minutes of his third game for England handed him the first major setback of his career. He still featured briefly for the national side in the European Championships, coming on as a substitute against Scotland.

Jamie Redknapp drives forward in a 1995 Premiership match with Newcastle. He made his Liverpool debut as an 18-year-old in 1991 but took another four years to mature into one of the finest midfielders in the country, blessed with eye-catching distribution and a fierce shot.

clocked up 90 matches, he only dominated games in fits and starts. That was only to be expected from a player who was thrown into the heated midfield action at Anfield before he was even out of his teens and, although Redknapp is just about the last player to be overawed by any on-field experience, his natural flair appeared inhibited by an over-reluctance to stray from the safety of Liverpool's laws of possession and simple passing. At that stage his most obvious qualities were the neatness and precision of his distribution, together with an unusual gift for giving the ball away only very rarely. The debit side of that account, however, showed that while his passes almost invariably found a red shirt, the recipient was rarely attacking a position of danger at the time; caution triumphed over daring and ambition.

Making advances

In the 1994-95 season, under the direct encouragement of Evans and his staff, Redknapp began to emerge from his shell and, starting from more advanced areas himself, began looking for defence-splitting passes. The increasing authority with which he performed was a massive influence on the Reds' success in the Coca Cola Cup that year. He also showed a willingness to provide the side with an alternative source of goals from midfield.

Jamie had proved himself one of the finest strikers of a dead ball in the league and began employing that power and accuracy in broken play as well. The most memorable goal of his campaign was the last-minute free-kick struck with venom and swerve to convince Blackburn momentarily that they had just lost the Championship, but the manner in which he opened the following term suggested that even better things were to come. He scored a vital UEFA Cup strike in Vladikavkaz with a dipping drive from all of 30 yards before hitting a controlled 20-yarder against Blackburn. His first 17 games brought him five goals in all.

Making a winning return

However, with conditions apparently set fair for Redknapp at club and international level, he found himself becalmed for four months by a hamstring strain suffered in the opening minutes of his third match for England, in November 1995. At first Liverpool struggled without him, but once Michael Thomas emerged as a tougher-tackling replacement the Reds embarked on an 18-match unbeaten run. That spell was ended by a defeat at Nottingham Forest that saw Redknapp recalled for the FA Cup semi-final against Aston Villa. Thomas had every right to be aggrieved by the decision but Redknapp's impressive response was to create two of the three goals that took Liverpool to Wembley. However, the holder of a record 18 England under-21 caps was in many observers' eyes fortunate to retain his place for the remainder of the season. And while Jamie did indeed look more like the cautious, lightweight tyro of his first Anfield outings than the confident, dynamic creator he had started to become before his injury, he was also suffering under the burden of expectation that his attitude, poise and rapid development into one of the country's top midfielders had generated.

Redknapp was robbed of an immediate chance to prove his detractors wrong by another injury suffered with England, this time in Euro '96, when he damaged an ankle. That problem, coupled with Thomas's form and the arrival of Patrik Berger, kept him on the bench for the early part of the 1996-97 campaign. The glee with which he celebrated a tap-in against Charlton on his return to the starting line-up showed how desperate he was to play, but an almost immediate recurrence of the ankle injury kept him out for another two months. When he did resume for the second half of the season Redknapp again took time to hit top form and his confidence began to suffer under the impatience of terrace taskmasters who would not have asked as much of any other 23-year-old.

Jamie Redknapp is not yet the complete midfielder; his left foot is still underemployed and he is more ball-playing artist than ball-winning artisan. Yet at the age of 24 there is no reason why he should be. Graeme Souness had not arrived at Anfield until he was almost 25, let alone held down a first-team place there since before his 20th birthday. Redknapp has the time and talent to complete the graduation from child prodigy to midfield mastermind. Despite a couple of unscheduled stops, he remains ahead of schedule.

Career History

Born: Barton-on-Sea, 25 June 1973
Signed: January 1991, from Bournemouth
Full debut: Auxerre 2 Liverpool 0, UEFA Cup, second round, first leg, 23 October 1991
Games: 209 (27 as sub)
Goals: 18

International Caps

Seven England caps

Honours

Coca-Cola Cup 1994-95

Other Clubs

Tottenham Hotspur, Bournemouth

Ian Rush

In 1967 Liverpool lined up a move for a young Bolton Wanderers striker by the name of Francis Lee, only to see Manchester City steal him from under their noses. A full 13 years later, while City were pondering the purchase of a young centre-forward from Chester called Ian Rush, the Reds repaid them for the earlier episode by nipping in to snatch the teenager's signature. In the following 15 years they never had to worry about where their next goal was coming from; the greatest British scorer of his era saw to that. Any doubts about his claims to that title are instantly dismissed by what becomes an exhausting flick through the record books. The short version is that Ian Rush, whose 47 strikes in 64 matches won him the Golden Boot, awarded to Europe's leading marksman, in 1984, is Liverpool's record overall

Ian Rush shows off the 1990 League Championship trophy. The contribution he made to his post-Juventus title was a more complete all-round one than had been seen in the four successes that preceded his move to Italy.

goalscorer. He has found the net more times in FA Cup matches, FA Cup finals and Merseyside derbies than any other 20th century player. No one owns more FA Cup winners' medals than the man from Flint, he is out on his own as a five-times winner of the League Cup and his 28 goals for Wales also constitutes a national record.

Passing up opportunities

Yet in his earliest days at Anfield, Rush gave not even the merest hint of the riches that were to lie ahead and so stumbling was the self-conscious 19 year old's initial form that many inside the club were readying themselves to write off the £300,000 that had made him the domestic game's most expensive teenager. The shy lad whose gangling awkwardness had seen him nicknamed 'Clanky' at Chester, where even after breaking into the first-team he still got ready for training in the apprentices' dressing room, struggled to fit in at his new club and seemed to have overdosed on the team-play principles of Liverpool's practice sessions, continually passing the ball when he could have had a shot himself. The problem was resolved by an unexpected meeting with Bob Paisley at which the player asked for a pay rise, only to be told by the manager that he

could only give him more money if he started scoring more goals and that if he didn't have a shot he would never be able to do that. Suitably focused, Rush began hitting the net

A despairing Kevin Ratcliffe can only watch as Rush blasts the ball past Everton's Bobby Mimms to seal victory with Liverpool's third goal – and his second – in the 1986 FA Cup final.

as though it was going out of fashion and was quickly into one of the longest runs of form in football history. He was handed a debut in place of the injured Kenny Dalglish in December 1980 but it was on his next appearance, when picked on merit to wear the number nine shirt in the following April's League Cup final replay, that he really served notice of his talent. Although the whippet-thin striker failed to score that night, he did rattle the West Ham crossbar and displayed the speed, anticipation and tenacity that would become synonymous with his game for the next decade and a half. Despite that promising beginning he was far from the finished article, being predominantly right-footed and relying more for scoring chances on his natural pace and shooting skills than on his close control. It is a tribute, therefore, to his aptitude and dedication on the training ground that within a couple of seasons no one could really remember which was his better foot and over time he became one of the finest receivers and shielders of a ball in the top flight.

In the years before he moved to Juventus for a single season his game was a more straightforward one as he hared through defences in pursuit of perfectly weighted through balls from Kenny Dalglish, as often as not skipping round the diving goalkeeper to slide the ball into

an empty net from the narrowest of angles. That made him top scorer in his first full season, a campaign in which he began what quickly took on the proportions of a personal vendetta against Everton, the team he had

After his return from Italy's Serie A, Ian Rush carried on against Everton where he had left off, by scoring twice against them in the 1989 FA Cup final. Here he celebrates the first goal, a strike that took him past Dixie Dean's derby scoring record.

supported as a boy, with his first goal against them. The following term he struck a derby record four times against them in a 5-0 win at Goodison en route to a second consecutive Championship that featured two further hat-tricks against Coventry and Notts County.

Already Rush was terrorising defences not only when he had the ball but also when he didn't: the tall striker quickly earned a reputation as his team's first line of defence, continually harrying and pressurising defenders into playing dangerous passes that would be gobbled up by the Reds' midfield. His work-rate was astounding. After pursuing the ball all the way across his opponents' back line until he finally forced a mistake, Rush would be instantly sprinting away into a position to receive yet another scoring pass, repeating the trick constantly through-out the 90 minutes.

Despite starting his last season at Anfield alongside Stan Collymore, Rush spent much of the season on the bench. However, he still stepped up to score several important goals and set a new record for scoring in FA Cup ties.

Continental jaunts

Perhaps his finest sustained exhibition of that talent came in Liverpool's march to the 1984 European Cup final, when Ian scored in the away leg of every round except, strangely, the opening 6-0 aggregate romp against Danish minnows BK Odense. The most important of those goals was the rare header that beat Atletico Bilbao, who had fancied their chances after returning from Anfield with a goalless draw, but his most virtuoso performance came in the 4-1 win at Benfica's famous Stadium of Light. To protect a slender first leg advantage, the Reds played Dalglish in a more withdrawn role and left Rush on his own up front. Quite apart from getting his name on the scoresheet once more, the Welshman singlehandedly tied up the entire Portuguese defence all night to disrupt their habit of building attacks methodically from the back.

Another coolly executed brace amid the hysterical hostility whipped up among Dinamo Bucharest's fanatical support for the semi-final second leg – his first finish a neat left-foot chip reminiscent of Dalglish's Champions' Cup winner of 1978 – took the Reds back to Rome, where Rush was once more on target in the penalty shoot-out to help win an unprecedented treble of trophies in the same season he was voted double Footballer of the Year.

If that had not alerted the continentals to his superhuman talent for goals then his contribution to Liverpool's historic League and FA Cup Double in the 1985-86 season certainly did. His 22 goals in 40 games fired his team to the title and the pair he saved for the Cup final win over Everton provided the outstanding memory of his year. Those goals – an acute angle finish from Molby's pass and a clinical volley from Whelan's deep cross – persuaded Juventus to make him their £3.2 million man, and a deal was agreed that allowed him to stay at Anfield for one more year before flying out to Turin. Everton probably wished he had gone straight away, for he left them with eight goals to remember him by in that season's five meetings with the Blues. The greyhound-paced striker signed off with a Kop-end winner against Watford in his last appearance for the Reds and made an emotional departure as he threw his jersey to the fans in rounding off his lap of honour.

Just over 12 months later, however, he was back. Unfortunate enough to find himself leading a Juve side that had failed to replace playmaker Michel Platini and was about to go into a decline that would see it go almost another decade without winning the Scudetto, Rushie was hampered by a nagging ankle injury and managed only eight goals in 29 appearances. That still made him top scorer by a street – his partner Michael Laudrup failed to register even once – but he was saddled with most of the criticism that accompanied the side's worst season since 1961-62 and the club elected to sell him back to Liverpool for £2.8 million.

Although his Italian adventure was widely seen as a personal disaster, Rush maintains it was the best move he ever made, as it gave him the chance to play against the greatest players in the world and improved his all-round game immeasurably. Anyone who saw the 'before' and 'after' versions of the player could not fail to agree. Although he did not score at anything like the rate of his first term he was, on his return, a far more complete footballer who could create for others and operate effectively outside the box as well as snaffle up any chance that came his way inside it.

He ended his first campaign back in the manner in which he had left, scoring twice against Everton at Wembley to win Liverpool the FA Cup, the second a perfect glancing header that belied his 'Toshack' nickname, awarded in ironic reference to the aerial ability of his great predecessor that he was almost completely lacking in his early days. His fifth goal in three winning FA Cup finals, against Sunderland in 1992, earned him another place in the record books.

During 1995-96, which was to be his last season at Anfield, he got his 42nd goal in the competition to beat Denis Law's 20th-century milestone and moved to within one strike of Geoff Hurst's top mark in the League Cup. Before then, however, Rush had experienced his proudest moment ever in the famous red when he lifted the Coca Cola Cup as captain to seal the team's revival under Roy Evans.

The 1996 FA Cup final could not provide Ian Rush with a fairytale ending but his place in Liverpool's history had already been long assured before he moved on to Leeds United in search of the regular Premiership football that he could no longer be guaranteed at Anfield. Sad to be leaving, and with a tear in his eye as he said his final goodbye to the Kop, Ian Rush took all his old ambition with him, aiming to take his career scoring total beyond the 400 mark and collect his outright record fourth FA Cup winners' medal. No one at Liverpool would bet against him doing exactly that.

Career History

Born: St Asaph, North Wales, 20 October 1961
Signed: April 1980, from Chester City, and August 1988, from Juventus
Full debut: Ipswich Town 1 Liverpool 1, Division One, 13 December 1980
Games: 649 (28 as sub)
Goals: 338

International Caps

73 Wales caps, 28 goals

Honours

European Cup 1983-84; League Championship 1981-82, 1982-83, 1983-84, 1985-86, 1989-90; FA Cup 1985-86, 1988-89, 1991-92; League Cup 1980-81, 1981-82, 1982-83, 1983-84, 1994-95

Other Clubs

Chester City, Juventus, Leeds United

Ian St John

'**E**xhibition football is all very well in its way,' said Ian St John soon after joining Liverpool in 1961, 'but give me football with a bite.' Over the rest of that decade, it was guaranteed that any game involving the little centre-forward would be played with the sharpest of edges. As ultra-competitive as his legendary manager, 'The Saint' brought to his new team a feisty blend of fire and finesse that would soon make him the scourge of defences from Portsmouth to Carlisle. That was his worth as an individual

The Saint dropped deeper during the second half of his Liverpool career and Emlyn Hughes credits the little Scot with teaching him the art of midfield play. Here, teacher shows pupil his skill at running with the ball.

and it was significant enough in its own right, but his contribution to the club's collective whole was of even greater value. For if there was one pivotal moment in the transformation of Liverpool FC from fallen giant to European colossus it has to be the signing of the fiery centre-forward from Motherwell for a club record £37,500. Not just because of the shining talent he brought to the team, but also because of what his arrival symbolised.

A serious piece of business

The purchase of St John for more than double the previous highest sum ever paid by the Anfield board showed to the players, the fans and the football world at large that after years of under-achievement, the Reds finally meant business, particularly as it was quickly followed by the £30,000 signing of Ron Yeats. Shankly knew that it was make-or-break time for Liverpool, and he made sure the directors knew it too. What they also knew was that had they not sanctioned the St John deal, their lack of ambition would probably have cost them the services of their manager, who was still fuming at their earlier refusal to finance a bid for the

The arrival of Ian St John in 1961 signalled the start of Bill Shankly's Anfield revolution. He scored regularly up front but his ability to create chances for others proved even more important to Liverpool's success.

prolific Brian Clough. The signing of 'The Saint', a newly capped Under-23 international, looked more of a gamble despite his cheaper price tag, but any boardroom misgivings would have been instantly laid to rest had they had the slightest inkling of the return that their stake was quickly going to reap.

Exhibition stuff

As it was, all sense of nervousness lasted less than the 90 minutes of St John's debut appearance for the club, which was made in what was ostensibly the type of 'exhibition foot-ball' for which he had so little time. In this instance though, the spice added to the final of the Liverpool Senior Cup by the fact that it was played against Everton was sufficient to inspire the little Scot into producing a performance that set the standards of commitment, skill and vision that he would live up to throughout his Anfield career. The Reds lost the tie 4-3, but all their goals were scored by Ian St John with the style and strength for which he would become famous. Standing just 5ft 8in tall and tipping the scales at 11st, the then 22 year old's lack of size never handicapped him for a second, because he always punched substantially more than his weight and packed more cunning and aggression into his squat frame than could many of the much bigger men he came up against.

Even his appearance and demeanour were more effective than many opponents' more conventional weapons, for the impish smile, the twinkle in his eye and the confident, strutting gait with which he carried himself on to the field suggested that he knew something his larger adversaries did not. The crowd loved him for it, and particularly for the way in which he demon-strated that he did indeed know plenty of things that the others did not.

That first game served the most emphatic of notices of the new boy's talent for goals but it did not even begin to hint at the partnership he would soon strike up with his attacking mate, Roger Hunt. Although returning totals of 18, 19 and 21 goals in his first three seasons, St John always played second fiddle to his comrade when it came to scoring, but made good the gap in the number of chances he created for him. Many of the finest examples in his own col-lection of goals came from headers. The Saint was phenomenal in the air, possessing immacu-late timing, the most springed of heels and the strength with which to bullet his efforts into the goal. Of all those strikes, the one that Liverpool fans will always remember with most affection was the flying, whiplash header that he hammered past Leeds United's Gary Sprake to win the FA Cup in 1965.

Revelling in the central role

By the time of that epic final, St John was beginning to find the target more infrequently, although his eye for an opportunity remained as sharp as ever. The difference now was that his talents were being employed in another area, and with even more devastating effect. Playing up front, the little striker displayed a unique combination of skill and steel, being blessed with the ability to outjump defenders in the air, outwit them on the ground and outthink them in his repertoire of subtle flicks and passes, and possessing the courage to put his foot or his head in where it really hurt. To observers from an earlier era, he reminded them of a more forceful and belligerent Albert Stubbins. From 1964-65 he paraded those talents from a deeper posi-tion in which he flourished, after first taking the role following an injury to Jimmy Melia. As the

The best remembered of all St John's goals is the flying header that won Liverpool their first FA Cup, in 1965. He is immortalised as 'Sinjin' by the commentator on the Pathe newsreel of the match.

focal point of the Liverpool attack, St John's skills of creation were now more vital than his prowess as a finisher, and even though he still loved to get forward as often as possible he thrived on that responsibility, threading balls through to his attackers and crafting openings for them with his vision and positional sense. His bustling aggression was still of use in battling for possession in his new role and that snapping tenacity and endless enthusiasm rarely endeared him to whichever opponent was detailed to keep tabs on him. While he was certainly hard-faced, St John was never a dirty player – although he did have a quick enough temper when riled – and was particularly touchy about suggestions that the abrasive edge to his game was more rough than tough, even going so far as to deny that his cropped hairstyle was an antisocial crewcut. His record backs up both the player's claims of being firm but fair and the opinion that his fuse was never the longest; his only booking in Scotland was rescinded on appeal, while his three sendings off for Liverpool were for retaliatory flare-ups.

Those explosions were mercifully rare, and the Reds always had more reason to be grateful for St John's toughness than cause to rue his pugnacity, particularly once they began coming up against the worldly wise continentals, against whom the little Scot grabbed ten goals in Anfield's first four European campaigns. He hit a vital strike in the 2-2 draw against Cologne in the 1965 European Cup quarter-final replay that Liverpool won on the toss of a disc, but the most rapturously received effort was the shot that rounded off the 3-1 home demolition of Inter Milan in the competition's last four.

Peaks and troughs

Like the whole of Bill Shankly's first great team, Ian St John was at his peak during those three heady seasons during the mid-1960s and as he entered his thirties during the latter years of that decade his form and fitness began to dip, until the end came – as it did for several other members of the side – with the shock FA Cup defeat at Watford in 1970.

The one opponent by which all footballers are eventually defeated, age, had finally taken the edge off St John's game, although there still remained the natural skill and the familiar determination and cussedness that Shankly had first seen in the young centre-forward he brought south from Motherwell, and who, in common with his mentor, ate, slept and drank the beautiful game. There have rarely been better judges of footballing class and character than the legendary Liverpool manager, and so there are few higher compliments that can be paid to Ian St John than the simple fact that he was the man whom Shankly chose to launch his Red revolution.

Career History
Born: Motherwell, 7 June 1938
Signed: May 1961, from Motherwell
Full debut: Liverpool 2 Bristol Rovers 0, Division Two, 19 November 1961
Games: 424 (five as sub)
Goals: 118

International Caps
21 Scotland caps, nine goals

Honours
League Championship 1963-64, 1965-66; FA Cup 1964-65

Other Clubs
Motherwell, Coventry City, Tranmere Rovers

Tommy Smith

It seems apt that Tommy Smith lost his chance to play in the 1978 European Cup final only by dropping an axe on his foot less than a fortnight before Liverpool were due to meet Bruges at Wembley. No doubt news of the garden accident prompted a few of his opponents to wonder whether he had started taking his work home with him: even though he was always more than merely a hatchet man, it is his physical approach to the game that will always be better remembered than the skill with which he could also perform. Such a reputation never really bothered its owner and the Reds have never had a more committed, determined and downright cussed servant than the tough little lad from Scotland Road who grew up to embody just about everything that Bill Shankly intended the institution he built to represent. Tommy joined the Anfield ground staff at the age of 15 and was deposited into the club's hands with a request from his mother for Shankly to look after him. Mrs Smith needn't have worried; for the better part of the next two decades it was her son who would be taking care of those around him in one sense, and those who threatened his team's goal in entirely another.

Doing things the hard way

His initial duties involved painting crush barriers on the Spion Kop terrace from which he had previously worshipped the Reds and he didn't go near a ball in his first two weeks. Once training was under way, however, he was so impressive that he found himself playing for the reserves – and alongside his idol Billy Liddell – almost straight away. Smithy's early progress created just as quickly the legendary tough streak that would earn him his title of the Anfield Iron as he decided that the best way to compensate for his lack of experience was to make his presence felt physically with consistently hard tackling. That philosophy seemed to work as he was handed his first-team debut when he was just 17. He persisted with the approach to make up for his lack of first hand knowledge of life in the top league. Tommy knew that his strength was, quite literally, his strength. Liverpool Catholic schools champion at both the high jump and the shot putt, it was the latter discipline that had most relevance to his football. The iron man actually began his senior

Liverpool career as a wing-half, but within six months of his debut he had found his spiritual home in the centre of defence. Operating first as 'Ron Yeats' right leg', then taking the leading role himself in the early 1970s, Tommy was one of the few constants in Shankly's two great sides and exuded a presence as colossal as that of the man he first learned his trade alongside.

Smith brings the ball out of defence against Leeds United at Anfield. The strong centre-half was never the quickest of defenders but his reading of the game and confident skills made up for that failing.

An honest man

Smithy always liked to describe himself as honest rather than hard, but his first manager's assertion that he had been quarried rather than born provides a truer measure of his toughness. The impact he made on Division One quickly earned him of an unsavoury reputation and he will admit to being 'a bit of a headcase' in his early years. By the time he succeeded Yeats as captain in 1970, he had calmed down significantly, partly as a result of having his social life regularly interrupted by local hard men asking him outside for a fight and partly through a new-found maturity in his all-round game. He was still no pussycat as he proved in his later assertion that: 'If I can shake a lad up with a good hard tackle early on then I'm made up because I know most of them won't be in much of a hurry for another one. They will be listening for me breathing down their neck.' Ossie Ardiles was one of the most famous recipients of such an introduction when Tommy welcomed him to these shores in 1978 with a jolting reminder that he couldn't 'expect not to be tackled just because Argentina won the World Cup'.

He also had the advantage of looking hard and the combination of his reputation and presence on the field meant that many of his battles were won without a shot being fired. He was one of the few players of whom opponents were actually scared. However, the fact that he was only ever sent off once – a dismissal for dissent, of all things, against Manchester City in 1973 – and managed successfully to avoid retribution to the point that he never had any of his own bones broken suggests that there was more to his game than brute strength and a bludgeon of a tackle. Smithy could not rely simply on speed to free him from sticky defensive situations. He was quite happy to describe himself as plain slow and prone to put on weight around his hips and backside, for he was confident in his class as a ball-player and reader of the game to compensate for those shortcomings. While he might not have been able to race back and halt an attacker who was about to shoot from the six-yard line, it was he who was most likely to pop up on exactly the right piece of goal line to thump that player's effort to safety.

Tommy's positional play enabled him to perform over an impressively lengthy period at the highest level without being embarrassed by his lack of pace. His good control, sound passing and measured excursions into enemy territory never went amiss either. His repeated appearance in the probing keep-ball of the Liverpool move that led to Kevin Keegan's second goal in the 1974 FA Cup final – a match played during the period in which he stood in admirably at right-back for the injured Chris Lawler – was particularly memorable, as he played a delicious one-two to create space for the low cross that picked out the number seven at the far post. By then Smithy was no longer captain, having been relieved of the position six months earlier after a row with Shankly over the manager's decision to drop him. The two strong-willed men enjoyed a good relationship, fashioned from the simple footballing philosophy they both shared. Sometimes, however, they turned the air between them blue. When they disagreed there was no way either party would think of backing down. But those bust-ups were quickly forgotten.

An outstanding final exit

The Anfield Iron never shouted less when he wasn't captain. With a bark as fierce as his bite, he continued bellowing his defence into line as the elder statesman of Bob Paisley's first teams. As the 1976-77 season began with Tommy in his 32nd year, Paisley let him know that he was unlikely to be more than a stand-in and Smithy announced he would hang up his boots at the campaign's end. But far from going out on a silent note he ended the campaign with the greatest moment of his career. An injury to Phil Thompson in March 1977 let the old faithful back in and he went with the side all the way to the European Cup final, in which he marked his 600th and supposedly last game for the club with the goal that gave the Reds the lead in the most important match of their history. Up for a corner and perhaps remembering his days as a schoolboy striker who was at his best in the air, Smithy soared unchallenged above the Mönchengladbach defence to head unstoppably into the net from the edge of the penalty area.

That ultimate fix of the Anfield drug to which he had been addicted all his life proved too strong a reminder of what he was about to walk away from and he stayed for another year, only this time his mishap with the axe prevented him from signing off in another blaze of glory, and he went quietly to John Toshack's Reds retirement home at Swansea City instead. Tommy Smith had given his all for Liverpool Football Club, and in skill, drive, commitment and the iron invincibility he gave his team's heart, his all was well nigh unmatchable.

Career History
Born: Liverpool, 5 April 1945
Signed: April 1962
Full debut: Liverpool 5 Birmingham City 1, Division One, 8 May 1963
Games: 633 (one as sub)
Goals: 48

International Caps
One England cap

Honours
European Cup 1976-77; UEFA Cup 1972-73, 1975-76; League Championship 1965-66, 1972-73, 1975-76, 1976-77; FA Cup 1964-65, 1973-74

Other Club
Swansea City

Graeme Souness

Whatever one looked for in a central midfielder, Graeme Souness had it, and the £352,000 Liverpool paid Middlesbrough for his services in 1978 effectively bought them several top-class players rolled into one. Peerless in his passing, his vision, his tackling and in his shooting from distance, he was simply the most complete player in his position that Anfield has ever seen and is ever likely to see. The freshness in the memory of the managerial misfortunes that befell both him and the club on his return to the famous stadium in 1991 will inevitably colour all perceptions of his overall contribution to the Reds' history but should never detract from the strutting splendour of the figure that was Souness the player in his magnificent, multi-talented pomp.

A hard reign

Intelligent and incisive, he was also one of the hardest men ever to play the game, as comfortable with the sledgehammer as he was with the scalpel, and it wasn't long before he revealed both sides of his imposing personality. Previous misdemeanours on Teesside meant that a couple of bookings picked up in his initial eight weeks at Anfield were enough to make him the first Liverpool player to be suspended for passing 20 disciplinary points in a single season, while just two months later he was calmly picking out the perfect pass for Kenny Dalglish to win the European Cup at Wembley.

Souness' potent brew always mixed eight parts good to two parts ugly, with only the most occasional dash of the bad thrown in, and to characterise him as simply a scowling assassin who happened to be able to play a bit is to underestimate him entirely. His creative talent was a far more important force than his appetite for destruction. For more than six years, he crafted the bullets with which the Reds' strikers fired the side

Graeme Souness was the most complete midfielder of his day – and he knew it. The imperious manner in which he ruled the centre of the pitch meant many of his battles were won before they had even started.

to glory at home and abroad, and he was the conduit through which all Liverpool's attacking movements flowed. The tough Scot was the heartbeat of some of the greatest of all Anfield outfits and his importance was summed up by manager Joe Fagan's belief that when Souness was missing, the team fired on only three cylinders. An elegant mover and a natural athlete, his quick footballing brain and instant ability to pick out the most dangerous pass on offer made him a perfect playmaker in the centre of the park, and he had both the control and

Souness powers away from Manchester United's Frank Stapleton at Wembley. The Scot's running with the ball and his shooting from distance were as forceful as his famed iron tackling.

the skill to execute those duties with unerring accuracy and consistency. 'Souey' may have lacked half a yard in pace, but his attacking play was otherwise faultless for he was as menacing moving forward with the ball at his feet as he was when spraying passes about the field to set the next attack in motion. He was a strong runner who was near-impossible to knock out of his stride and once his smooth-flowing action had carried him to within sight of the goalposts he never hesitated to unleash one of the most powerfully precise finishes in the game.

Souness could not only pick his spot from almost any position around the edge of the box but could also find that chosen target with scorching pace. He hit a searing hat-trick against CSKA Sofia en route to the 1980-81 European Cup triumph and rocketed his penalty in the 1984 final's shoot-out unstoppably into the roof of the Roma net, but perhaps the high-profile goal that best combined those two qualities was the strike that defeated Everton in the replay of the 1984 Milk Cup final. Souness ran on to the ball outside the box and let fly with a 20-yarder that went no more than a couple of inches above the turf to scream inside Neville Southall's left-hand post by a similar margin, the velocity and trajectory of the shot giving the Blues' keeper no chance whatsoever.

The cold hard facts

However, the triple European Cup winner's creative bent could never have existed solely in splendid isolation, and much of his attacking dynamism derived from the mean streak that dominated the darker side of his personality. The cold steel Souness brought to his play was a physical expression of his phenomenal will to win and without such strength of character he would never have been the complete midfielder that he was.

As competitive in training as he was when cups and titles were at stake, his determination and self-belief, which bordered on the arrogant, gave him an aura of serene invincibility which was as important a part of his make-up as his ball skills and tackling power. Indeed, his team-mates observed that he never had to make as many tackles as other players: his strength of presence invariably turned what would have been 50-50 challenges for lesser men into confrontations that were weighted 80-20 in his favour. In view of the crunching power with which his tackles were executed that was unsurprising, but Souness was never really the cynical bruiser his critics liked to portray him as. Encroaching age and a misguided belief in the necessity of proving his toughness meant his final playing days in Scotland – a country that had never given its prodigal son the praise to which he felt he was entitled, thanks to his form in the dark blue jersey rarely matching that for his club – were characterised by wincingly late assaults and more cards than a marathon whist drive, yet before moving from Sampdoria to Rangers he had been sent off only twice.

Lasting memories

Perhaps that figure should really have been a little bit higher, but Souness was wise enough to commit to memory affronts for which he would extract stealthy retribution at a later date. Craig Johnston likened him to a protective big brother who would sort out anyone he caught taking liberties with his weaker siblings, and that analogy was not too far off the mark. Taking liberties with the man himself, however, was even more dangerous than roughing up his team-mates, as Dinamo Bucharest midfielder Lica Movila discovered to his cost in the European Cup

A delighted Souness lifts the European Cup in his last match for Liverpool, the 1984 European Cup final in Rome. In his three seasons as captain, the midfielder also collected a further three League Championships and three League Cups.

semi-final of 1984. Movila spent most of the first leg at Anfield kicking, punching and tugging at the shirt of his opponent, before he unexpectedly departed with his jaw broken in two places by a lightning strike from a Souness elbow that was witnessed by the entire Main Stand but none of the officials. The reception that act earned the Scotsman in the return might have fazed many a less self-assured individual, but it served only to inspire the Liverpool captain to a compelling display of style and swagger that took his team through to the final. Spotting that the entire stadium was booing every touch that he made during the pre-match kick-in, his team-mates gradually formed a circle around him from which they raised the cacophony of disapproval to a shrieking crescendo by passing only to the man in the middle. Then, at precisely the right moment, Souness sold 60,000 Romanians one of the sweetest dummies of his career to stop them sheepishly in mid-boo, before going on to completely dominate the game itself and create the Ian Rush goals that sent the Reds on to Rome.

That style extended to the off-field life he lived in the manner that earned him his Champagne Charlie nickname, although it was only in the first two weeks of his time at Anfield that his bar bill came close to exceeding the cost of his hotel room. Always immaculately dressed and groomed regardless of the hour at which he had returned home the previous night, Souness was even reputed to put his underwear on hangers. He once showed that he could still cut a dignified figure even without the expensive tailoring success had bought him. After David Hodgson had stolen his trousers during a pre-season tour, he calmly stepped on to the plane home wearing a borrowed overcoat from beneath which protruded only his hairy legs and black socks. Such was his poise and self-assurance – only Souness could have roamed the streets of Liverpool at night calling out for a missing family dog by the name of Cuddles without fear of ridicule – that nobody felt inclined to ridicule his state of undress. That was no surprise; a bigger one was that Hodgson had dared carry out such a venture in the first place.

The main man

On the pitch, however, Souness was never caught with his trousers down and was equally loathe to allow any outside factors to interfere with his game. Liverpool's most successful skipper was a born winner and he led his team by the shining example of determination and indestructible will to win that he set himself. Those qualities, coupled with the tenacity, skill and sweeping vision with which he played made him almost unbeatable. His is the standard against which all Liverpool midfielders have to be judged.

Career History

Born: Edinburgh, 6 May 1953
Signed: January 1978, from Middlesbrough
Full debut: Liverpool 1 West Bromwich Albion 0, Division One, 14 January 1978
Games: 352 (two as sub)
Goals: 56

International Caps

54 Scotland caps, three goals

Honours

European Cup 1977-78, 1980-81, 1983-84; League Championship 1978-79, 1979-80, 1981-82, 1982-83, 1983-84; League Cup 1980-81, 1981-82, 1982-83, 1983-84

Other Clubs

Tottenham Hotspur, Middlesbrough, Sampdoria, Glasgow Rangers

Albert Stubbins

The toss of a coin decided Liverpool's European fate on several occasions during the 1960s, but it was the spin of another disc just a few weeks into the 1946-47 season that brought the first postwar Championship to Anfield. For the prize in that lottery, held in the Newcastle United boardroom, was the services of Albert Stubbins, whose 24 goals in the 36 games that followed his move to Merseyside fired the Reds to their first League title in more than 20 years. Yet had the coin landed the other way up, wartime football's leading goalscorer would have found himself heading for, of all places, Goodison Park.

Stubbins, then 27 and desperate for First Division football, had asked for a move away from Newcastle to realise that aim, and his appearance on the transfer list sparked interest from Liverpool, Everton and 12 other top flight clubs. Both Merseyside outfits agreed to pay £13,000 – then the second highest transfer fee in league history – for the red-haired centre-forward, and Newcastle's directors left the final decision on which side to join to the player himself. However, Stubbins could not be found and the bidders were kept waiting for five and a half hours until their unwitting quarry was alerted to the pursuit by a message flashed up on a cinema screen as he sat watching a newsreel. On arriving at St James' Park, the England inter-national could not decide which manager to speak to first, and tossed a coin to settle the matter. It came down heads for Liverpool, and a deal was struck in a matter of minutes because in the negotiations Stubbins' main concern was in fact not the money on offer. While at Newcastle he had written a weekly column in the local evening newspaper and, keen to move on to a career in journalism once his playing days were over, now asked for the guaran-tee of a similar job on Merseyside. Reds' manager George Kay agreed immediately, the deal was sealed and Stubbins was left only to tell Everton boss Theo Kelly that he had agreed to move to the Anfield side of Stanley Park.

Childhood promise

That was in September 1946, and the strong, skilful striker was quick to give the fans a taste of the talent that had marked him out as a footballing prodigy at the age of five, when he was able to keep the ball up for more than a minute using only his head and could trap it stone dead with either foot. A fine passer and intelligent reader of the game, his career statistics tell only half the story of his contribution to the Liverpool cause, as Stubbins created as many goals as he scored during his seven-year spell at Anfield. He wasted no time in opening his account for the Reds, netting on his debut at Bolton Wanderers, but fans on the Kop had to endure a longer wait for Albert's first strike at Anfield. And before that goal arrived, in his fourth home game, a 1-0 win over Brentford, they witnessed what Stubbins still looks back on as one of his lowest moments in the red shirt. The tall striker had been Newcastle's regular penalty taker for most of his time at St James' and possessed a proud record of never having missed from the spot. On his second appearance at Anfield, against Leeds United, he was brought down in the box and instinctively rose to take the resulting penalty himself. He struck the kick with accuracy and venom but saw his effort foiled by a fine save from the goalkeeper,

Albert Stubbins was the second most expensive buy in football history when he joined Liverpool in 1946. The Reds received an immediate return on their investment when the striker's goals won them the Championship that same season.

whose arm was broken in the process by the sheer force of the shot. Despite the excellence of the save, Stubbins always counted that incident as a miss on his part, and he was never asked to take another penalty in competitive action for the Reds. Ironically, the only other spot kick that he took for Liverpool was in a friendly against Newcastle United and he missed that too, this time firing his shot over the bar. Yet neither of those misses affected Stubbins, and he would have been more than happy to take on the responsibility once more at any time. That was a measure of the confidence which made him such a fine finisher and a true hero of the Kop.

A confident all-rounder

The Geordie's intelligence shone through in his passing and movement on the pitch, whether in creating space for himself or in spotting and finding a team-mate in a more dangerous position, but it was the conviction of his shooting that made him one of the deadliest finishers of his day. Stubbins played with the belief that every shot he struck was goalbound and to this day he still attributes his impressive strike rate to that self-assurance. Unburdened by any fear of failure, the sure-footed striker's nervelessness and appetite for goals had made him the perfect penalty taker – that Anfield miss notwithstanding – and his confidence in front of the posts was never better demonstrated than in one particular representative match played during his Liverpool career. Appearing for the English League in a game against the Irish League during the late 1940s, his side were awarded three penalties during the 90 minutes. England were captained that day by Raich Carter, who was well known for his own success rate from the spot, but it was Stubbins whom the skipper invited to take the first that day. The Liverpool man blazed his effort over the bar, only to find himself summoned once more the next time the referee pointed to the spot. This time, the goalkeeper saved, but soon after another English player was fouled inside the box. Again, Stubbins was called forward and this time he shot sweetly into the net with none of the self-doubt that for lesser men would have been the legacy of those two earlier misses. As if to emphasise that confidence, Albert said of the episode: 'It wouldn't have bothered me if I had missed three in the game and been asked to take a fourth.'

Although blessed with the self-belief needed by all strikers, whose careers will forever be measured in the black and white of goals per game statistics, Stubbins' brimming confidence never spilled over into arrogance. Quite the reverse in fact; his skill on the pitch was exceeded only by his modesty off it, where he always sought to play down his own achievements in favour of those of the entire team.

A long-lasting individual contribution

Stubbins was also of a different breed to the thud and blunder battlers who had led the forward lines of pre-war football, and to a large extent changed the way Liverpool played through his thoughtful approach to the game. On the last day of the Reds' 1946-47 campaign, a win at fellow title chasers Wolves was needed to bring the Championship to Anfield, provided Stoke City lost at Sheffield United a fortnight later. Results duly went Liverpool's way and so the pre-planned Albert Stubbins goal that gave his side a 2-1 win at Molyneux was the one that won the League. Before kick-off, Stubbins had asked winger Bob Priday to drop deep and try to knock the ball long over Wolves defender Stan Cullis' head for him to chase. Priday did just that, and according to Stubbins he 'just managed to get between the full-backs' and then 'just managed to push the ball past the goalkeeper and into the net'. What really happened was that Stubbins collected Priday's pass inside the centre circle and raced almost half the length of the pitch, beating two covering defenders, before calmly sliding the ball beyond the keeper's reach with the perfect finish. It was a goal good enough to win any Championship, but to the ever-modest Stubbins it was no better than his simplest tap-in.

Memorable moments

That season, Stubbins also displayed his bravery in scoring one of the finest hat-tricks ever to have been seen at Anfield, against Birmingham City in a snowbound FA Cup tie. The striker always rated his second goal as the best, but his third is the one that stuck in the memory: he flung himself full length to head Billy Liddell's thunderous free-kick into the net before losing almost all the skin off his knees to the frozen pitch as he landed. And if that was not painful enough, he also received an unheard-of kiss on the cheek from his captain, Phil Taylor, to mark his feat! After that momentous beginning, the fortunes of both Liverpool and Stubbins – who, as the favourite footballer of John Lennon's father, was pictured on the cover of the Beatles' *Sergeant Pepper's Lonely Hearts Club Band* album in 1967 – began to decline.

Although he continued to score regularly when fit, Albert was increasingly plagued by injury trouble in his latter years at Anfield. After a long-running, impenetrable wrangle over money and his newspaper column that saw him miss the beginning of several successive seasons, the two eventually parted company in 1953.

Career History

Born: Wallsend, 13 July 1919

Signed: September 1946, from Newcastle United

Full debut: Bolton Wanderers 1 Liverpool 3, Division One, 14 September 1946

Games: 180

Goals: 83

Honours

League Championship 1946-47

Other Club

Newcastle United

Peter Thompson

As a schoolboy full-back in his native Carlisle, Peter Thompson was once dropped from his team for dribbling too much. By the end of his first season at Anfield, spectators could not get enough of his fancy footwork and attacking zeal, because it was the addition of Thompson's graceful wing-play to an already impressive Liverpool line-up that turned the side from title hopefuls in their first season back in the top flight to champions of England by the end of their second. The Kop called him 'The Magician' and not without good reason, as the dancing winger left opponent after opponent spellbound by his bewitching ball skills to create chance after chance for Roger Hunt and Ian St John. So elusive was he that after one match against Manchester United in which he had given full-back Paul Edwards a humiliating chasing, Wilf McGuinness felt the need to introduce his defender to the man he had been trying to mark, as he hadn't managed to get close enough to Thompson to even say hello.

Managers rarely tire of insisting they are just a player away from having a Championship-winning side, but as the 1962-63 season headed towards its conclusion Bill Shankly would have been quite justified in voicing such an opinion. He knew that the missing man was Peter Thompson and so unshakeable was his belief in that fact that he was prepared to spend a club record £40,000 to beat off the challenges of Juventus, Everton, Wolves and Hull, who were all coming to similar conclusions.

A solid background

Peter had the perfect pedigree for Shankly, had succeeded Tom Finney, the idol of Preston North End and the player the Liverpool boss rated above all others, as a 17 year old and had looked a worthy heir in the process. The promise he showed at Deepdale was quickly fulfilled at Anfield, where in tandem with Ian Callaghan on the opposite flank he helped create the most exciting wing partnership in the domestic game. The pair's contrasting styles complemented each other perfectly – Callaghan the more direct of the two, Thompson the trickier – and gave Liverpool a whole new range of options. Everton legend Dixie Dean was even

Peter Thompson was arguably the most skilful Liverpool player of his era. Tired team-mates would be instructed by Shankly to give the winger the ball and have a rest while he beat a selection of opponents.

Peter Thompson's brand of wing-play was based on a combination of speed, strength and unanswerable skill. Unlike many other artistic entertainers, Peter possessed the ability to sustain his standards throughout the 90 minutes of a match.

moved to observe that had he had the opportunity of feeding off their crosses then he would have shattered his own record of 60 goals in a season.

Thompson was one of football's true entertainers and one of the most naturally gifted ball players Anfield has seen. Shankly ranked him among the greatest of all the club's servants and hailed him as the most unstoppable winger he had come across. While Peter preferred to jink and dummy his way past bamboozled defenders with an illusionist's sleight of foot, he also possessed a raw strength that enabled him to muscle his way out of the tightest of corners whenever the need arose. An individualist who would win matches almost single-handedly, he could occasionally be a frustratingly mercurial performer prone to prolonging the full-back's agony when an early cross might have caused his opponents more collective pain.

Critical voices

The other most common complaints about his game voiced from the terraces and the sports pages were that for all his flair he did not score enough goals and his crossing was too inconsistent. Even Bill Shankly had to admit that these charges were not without foundation, but he pointed out in his player's defence that few other wingers caused as much indirect damage as did Peter Thompson. In his style and stamina he defied the stereotype of the artistic wingman who went missing when the going got tough and drifted in and out of games as the mood took him. Peter had an engine that kept him motoring up and down the flank for the duration and made up in volume for what some of his centres may have lacked in direction. His relatively modest goals return, however, proved a more intractable problem as the blistering pace of his shots was never really matched by a similarly high level of accuracy. That is not to say that he was any real sort of liability in front of goal, for he scored a fair number of spectacular and important strikes. In the former bracket, few of his finishes were ever more stunning than the one with which he graced the first ever match of the 1960s to be televised in colour. Thompson thumped in a left-foot shot on the West Ham goal, only to see the ball rebound straight back to him off an upright. While most other players would have been caught out by the unexpected bounce, Peter's skill and presence of mind allowed him to control the ricocheting ball in an instant and knock it smartly into the net with his right. And of the timeliest of occasions on which he graced the score-sheet, the most merited came with the brace he bagged during the Thompson-inspired 5-0 drubbing of Arsenal that clinched the 1963-64 League Championship.

That was a fitting climax to a fantastic first term at Anfield for Thompson, which from his debut against Blackburn, when he tore the Rovers defence to shreds, had marked him out as a special talent. Peter had already won international recognition while at Deepdale, but despite his continued fine form at Anfield he won only a comparatively meagre total of 16 caps for his country. The situation was largely a legacy of Alf Ramsey's decision to dispense with wingers from 1966 onwards, although the England manager did pay the Liverpool man the compliment of being the only orthodox wide man named among the initial party of 28 that travelled to Mexico for the 1970 World Cup. The broader, free-roving commission that Shankly had handed Thompson the previous season may have reawakened Ramsey's interest, but in the end all it earned him was the chance to make up the numbers in training at that tournament.

Lighting up the continent

Peter enjoyed greater international recognition at club level and although he had slipped out of the first-team before Liverpool's first European trophy arrived at Anfield he had already made his name as an integral part of the 1960s side that went so close to triumph in the 1964-65 European Champions' Cup and the following season's European Cup-Winners' Cup. His swaying runs and dancing feet lodged so firmly in the continental consciousness that as late as the 1970-71 campaign – his last season of regular action – Dinamo Bucharest captain Corneliu Dinu was convinced that to stop the Reds' Fairs Cup progress: 'We must annihilate Thompson.' The Romanians would have had to catch him first, and failed on all counts, going out of the competition by a 4-1 aggregate. By then, however, Peter's Anfield career was about to hit the downward slope. A cartilage injury began to cause him long-term problems which allowed Steve Heighway to take his place in the team.

A substitute's appearance in the 1971 FA Cup final proved to be his last chance on the big stage. By 1973 doctors gave him only another 12 months in which to play. That he went on to give another four seasons of outstanding service to Bolton Wanderers says much for the strength of character that would have marked him out from so many other twinkle-toed wide men even if his talent had been only the equal of theirs. But as his legion of Anfield admirers were always well aware, the range of skills Peter Thompson had at his disposal always put him in a league of his own.

Career History

Born: Carlisle, 27 November 1942
Signed: August 1963, from Preston North End
Full debut: Blackburn Rovers 1 Liverpool 2, Division One, 24 August 1963
Games: 412 (eight as sub)
Goals: 54

International Caps

16 England caps

Honours

League Championship 1963-64, 1965-66; FA Cup 1964-65

Other Clubs

Preston North End, Bolton Wanderers

Phil Thompson

Few Liverpool players possess a finer Anfield pedigree than Phil Thompson, and fewer still can ever have worn the famous red jersey with more pride. The first game he was taken to as a skinny 11 year old from Kirkby was the famous European Cup defeat of Inter Milan, after which he began making regular but brief visits to the Boys' Pen on the Kop, as he and his mates would hop over into the main body of the heaving terrace, where they preferred to strain for a view instead.

A flying start to lengthy success

He joined the club as an apprentice who was given five bob a week by Ian Callaghan and Emlyn Hughes for cleaning their boots, signed professional forms on his 17th birthday, helped the Reds' junior side to the final of the FA Youth Cup a year later and went on to make an impressive debut for the first team within another six months. That initial 1972-73 season earned him an unusual double of winners' medals from the League Championship and, slightly less glamorously, the Central League. Within seven years he was club captain and quickly led his men to a pair of First Division titles and a European Cup success in just under three campaigns in his charge. In all he won 13 major honours in his 11-year senior career at Anfield and later returned for a further six years as reserve team coach, grooming for stardom such talents as Steve McManaman and Robbie Fowler.

'Tommo', as he was known to the Kop, learned his skills on the streets of Kirkby, kicking around a cheap plastic football that was deemed too expensive to replace and instead had to be repaired with a red hot poker whenever it burst. And so keen on the game was he that when his class were asked to write diaries of what they did outside school, Phil made things up because he didn't think the teacher would believe that he devoted every spare minute to playing football.

Always a model professional, he never lost that dedication or love of the game in general and of Liverpool FC in particular. Without those traits and a similar level of determination, he might never have made it to the very top of his profession for he needed such attributes to compensate for a physique more suited to impersonating Olive Oyl than playing top class football. Standing six feet tall, he had filled out to all of 10st 7lb by the end of his first full season, 1973-74, having struggled to top nine stones when he first joined the club. But whether playing in midfield, where he began his career, or after moving to centre-back following an injury to Larry Lloyd in the latter part of 1973, he competed with a rare passion and determination that made light of his frail frame.

A defensive move

Bill Shankly was always greatly tickled by the wafer-thin figure who had come up through the ranks – he used to claim that Phil had tossed up with a sparrow for legs and lost – yet he knew that the player would never let him down in even the toughest of situations. That faith led the manager to put Tommo in at centre-back after the injury to Lloyd, surprising no one more than the then 19 year old himself. It turned out to be another inspired masterstroke as Phil went on to form two of the club's finest-ever defensive partnerships, playing alongside first Emlyn Hughes and then Alan Hansen.

In both pairings, Phil tended to take responsibility for dealing with high balls while the other man covered the floor around him. That combination accounted twice in quick succession for the much touted Malcolm Macdonald in 1974, first at St James' Park and then at Wembley in the FA Cup final, the match that really heralded the new man's defensive coming of age. Yet he was as much at home playing on the deck as in the air, and in later years, while Hansen's regular safaris into uncharted territory beyond the halfway line might have often overshadowed his team-mate's more straightforward creativity, Tommo's accurate distribution and preference for playing his way out of defence rather than simply clearing for distance set Liverpool on the attack with equal regularity.

Mixing brains and brawn

Although never any sort of goalscorer, he was a thoughtful, constructive type of player, whose outstanding reading of the game always gave him the time to select the most positive option when in possession and the foresight to be able to make life as awkward for an attacker as possible when the opposition had the ball. His lanky, raw-boned figure never allowed him to appear quite the most elegant of tacklers or headers – particularly when performing alongside Hansen's stylish action – but he could dump his adversaries on the deck with unexpected vigour and was blessed with single-minded determination in the air.

Such levels of commitment were the Thompson hallmark and, quite apart from seeing him battle back from two career-threatening cartilage operations, did as much as anything to endear him to the fans. Driven on by his pride in representing the club and in his desire for the team to succeed he was an example and inspiration to those around him and was the obvious heir to the captaincy when Emlyn Hughes began to drop out of the picture in the late 1970s.

Phil had missed out on the 1977 European Cup final through injury, and confessed to feeling pangs of jealousy at seeing Hughes hold aloft the trophy both that year and at Wembley 12 months later. In 1981, however, he realised his ambition of lifting club football's greatest prize after the 1-0 defeat of Real Madrid in Paris to crown his honour-strewn career. In 1979 he had been the first Liverpool-born player to captain England, but arguably the more intoxicating

Thompson clears from Manchester City's Joe Royle in 1976. The tall centre-back was always a sterner tackler than his angular frame suggested and he used the ball constructively when it was at his feet.

experience of that year was the day on which he fulfilled a lifelong ambition by leading his club side out at Anfield for the very first time. As a joke, his team-mates all followed him out of the dressing room before stopping in the tunnel so that Tommo emerged on his own and set off to wave as usual to his brother on the Kop with no sign of his team-mates behind him. Unfortunately, the gag was lost on the new skipper as he was so overcome by the emotion of his moment that he didn't even realise what had happened until he was brought up to date with those earlier events after the final whistle.

The pride he took in captaining the Reds was fired by his natural bond with their constituency of the Kop and he never lost touch with those roots. As an FA Cup winner in 1974 he was still sharing a room with his brother at the family home in Kirkby, where he also ran a Sunday league team while playing for Liverpool, and a homecoming Anfield photocall for the European Cup was once slightly delayed while Phil retrieved the trophy from behind the bar of his local pub, where his friends, family and an endless stream of children were having their pictures taken with it!

An outstanding defence

Being handed the Liverpool captaincy in April 1979 was the peak of a season in which Tommo's Liverpool reached new heights by conceding a total of just 16 goals in 42 league games, an achievement that he ranks as just about the finest of that team's amazing feats. But by December of 1981 Phil was no longer captain as Bob Paisley elected to relieve him of the job in an effort to help him overcome an atypical spell of desperately inconsistent form. He was naturally upset by the decision, but it seemed to do the trick as he came back in typical point-proving fashion to earn his Championship medal and play well enough to represent England in Spain during the 1982 World Cup.

That was his last full term as a Red: the following season another serious injury gave Mark Lawrenson the chance to make the second centre-back job his own, an opportunity he grasped firmly. Tommo moved on for a couple of seasons at Sheffield United before Kenny Dalglish brought him on to the backroom staff in 1986 for a six-year stint of making as whole-hearted a contribution to the club's future as he had to its past. Although no longer involved at Anfield, the example of loyalty and endeavour that Phil Thompson set stands as an object lesson to all hopefuls who look to Liverpool's history for inspiration.

Career History

Born: Liverpool, 21 January 1954
Signed: January 1971
Full debut: Norwich City 1 Liverpool 1, Division One, 28 October 1972
Games: 466 (seven as sub)
Goals: 12

International Caps

42 England caps, one goal

Honours

European Cup 1977-78, 1980-81; UEFA Cup 1975-76; League Championship 1972-73, 1975-76, 1976-77, 1978-79, 1979-80, 1981-82, 1982-83; FA Cup 1973-74; League Cup 1980-81, 1981-82

Other Club

Sheffield United

John Toshack

John Toshack's achievements as a manager in Spain and Portugal have made him a hero on the continent, but in his playing days the tall, strong Welshman was just about the last man that overseas sides wanted to see lining up against them. Many of the multi-talented forward's finest hours in the red of Liverpool came during their conquest of Europe in the 1970s. An achilles tendon injury forced him to miss the unforgettable night in Rome on which the Champions' Cup came to Anfield for the first time, but by then he had already made his mark on one international club final. Bill Shankly described Toshack as 'an essential in modern football', and the legendary manager never found him more indispensable than on the night of the 1973 UEFA Cup final first leg at Anfield – an occasion on which his centre-forward wasn't even in the team.

Torrential rain forced the abandonment of the match against Borussia Mönchengladbach that evening, but in the period of play that had taken place Shankly saw that the German defence was vulnerable in the air. For the re-arranged game played 24 hours later, he brought in the towering Toshack for the diminutive Brian Hall. The ploy worked wonderfully, with the then 24 year old winning cross after cross to set up chances for his fellow forwards. Kevin Keegan tucked away two Toshack flick-ons and defender Larry Lloyd also got on the scoresheet to help the side to a 3-0 win that proved just enough – after they had lost the second leg 2-0 – to land Liverpool their first ever European trophy.

Expert tuition from a master footballer

John Toshack had joined Liverpool from Cardiff City in November 1970 for £110,000. At the age of just 21, a youngster he may have been, but raw and untested at the highest level he certainly was not. Tutored at Ninian Park by the great John Charles, Toshack was already an established Welsh international before his move to Anfield and had also played 19 times in Europe, scoring 11 goals in those games. But it was the 100 occasions on which he struck for

his club in around twice that number of match-
es that really impressed, to such an extent that
Liverpool's watching chief scout, Geoff
Twentyman, enthused in his notebook that
Toshack was 'ready for the First Division now'.

And indeed he was. His debut in a 0-0
Anfield draw against Coventry City may not have
stuck in anyone's memory – the man himself
says of the occasion: 'I don't remember too
much about it, which probably means I didn't
have a good game!' But his second appearance, in a home fixture against Everton, certainly did. With 21 minutes to play, Everton had
a 2-0 lead. Then Steve Heighway pulled one
back for Liverpool before Toshack earned himself an instant elevation to the pantheon of the
Kop, outjumping Brian Labone to head the Reds
back on terms before winning the flick-on from
which Chris Lawler snatched a stirring victory
just before the end. The 6ft 2in striker gave
early warning of his aerial prowess in that most
famous of derbies, but several more seasons would pass before his all-round skills
truly began to bloom. In fact, the big man's
first term at Anfield ended on a disappoint-

*John Toshack moves on to a through ball with Peter
Cormack in close support. While the Welsh giant was
famed for his ability in the air, he was also an intelligent
user of the ball on the floor.*

ing note as his own supply of goals dried up and his youthful Liverpool team eventually bowed
to the experience of Arsenal's Double winners in extra-time during the 1971 FA Cup final.

Watching from the Wembley stands that day was Bill Shankly's latest signing, a certain
centre-forward by the name of Kevin Keegan, who over the next six years would form with
Toshack the most potent attacking combination in English – and arguably European – football.
So intuitive was their partnership that each player's name is even now still synonymous with
that of the other, yet the popular recollection of the giant Toshack continually knocking down
high balls for his sharp, terrier-like comrade to tuck away does the Welshman a disservice. For
John Toshack was a far more complete footballer than he is often given credit for. Bill Shankly,
for one, recognised that and so in dubbing him one of the modern game's 'essentials', he was
at pains to add: 'And that covers all aspects of his play.'

A winning mentality

Quiet and unassuming, the player who published a volume of his poetry entitled *Gosh, it's Tosh*
was never one to blow his own trumpet, but the intelligence that has made him so successful
in management was always on show in his performances on the pitch. Although his main
goalscoring fame was as a header of the ball, most of those finishes were cleverly placed
beyond the goalkeeper's reach rather than simply blasted towards the target. On the floor, he

also showed good ball control and the distribution to capitalise on his awareness of his team-mates' whereabouts. His dummy runs and ability to draw defenders out of position were as effective in creating chances for Keegan as was the Welshman's dominance in the air.

Toshack's determination on the field rarely manifested itself in either aggression or retaliation, and he preferred to prove himself through deeds rather than words in working his way back from whatever problems he faced. When dropped by Shankly in December 1971, he responded by hitting six goals in three reserve games. That was the sort of dedication that enabled him to keep secret for four months of the 1972-73 season the leg injury that eventually forced him to re-evaluate his whole style of play, and it was only in the April that his dipping form finally forced him to come clean. But the cause of his problem remained a mystery until Bob Paisley decided to sell him to Leicester City for £160,000 in November 1974, only for the deal to be scuppered by a medical examination that pinpointed the problem in his thigh.

His career was thought to be effectively finished by that verdict, but his determination and a switch in style gave him another three seasons as a key Liverpool player. In fact, the season after the injury was diagnosed he played more games than ever before, notching up a half century of appearances to set alongside a best-ever goals return of almost one every two games. Working closely with Bob Paisley in tactical sessions that whetted his appetite for management, Toshack concentrated on honing his positional play and reading of the game in order to reduce the amount of flat-out sprinting to which his leg was subjected. Heavy pitches became his worst enemy, and the tip-toeing style of running he evolved made him most effective on hard ground.

The Reds again lifted the UEFA Cup in May 1976, a personal triumph for Toshack. Substituted as his side went 2-0 down in the first leg of the final, at home to Bruges in a match they then fought back in to win 3-2, he bounced back immediately to score in the League title-clinching win at Wolves and then play his full part in the 1-1 second-leg draw in Belgium that won Liverpool the UEFA Cup. But his exertions that term took their toll. He was still feeling the effects of that marathon campaign more than a year later as the 1977-78 season began.

With those fitness problems still hanging over him and renewed competition for places from the likes of Kenny Dalglish, David Fairclough and David Johnson, John Toshack jumped at the chance to take his first step into management at Swansea City. That move back to his native Wales began a second career that, with Sporting Lisbon, Real Sociedad, Real Madrid and Deportivo La Coruna has already garnered him almost as many honours as he won in his playing days at Anfield.

Career History
Born: Cardiff, 22 March 1949
Signed: November, 1970
Full debut: Liverpool 0 Coventry City 0, Division One, 14 November 1970
Games: 245 (nine as sub)
Goals: 95

International Caps
40 Wales caps, 13 goals

Honours
UEFA Cup 1972-73, 1975-76; League Championship 1972-73, 1975-76, 1976-77; FA Cup 1973-74

Other Clubs
Cardiff City, Swansea City

Paul Walsh

Some players are born great, some achieve greatness and some have greatness thrust upon them. Others, including the unfortunate Paul Walsh, have greatness snatched from their grasp by the cruellest of fates. The little Londoner arrived at Anfield, a couple of weeks before the Reds lifted their fourth European Cup in May 1984, as the most sought-after 21 year old in British football and the obvious successor to Kenny Dalglish. Voted Young Player of the Year shortly before his £700,000 move from Luton, he was hugely promising, but a heart-breaking succession of serious injuries sustained over the next four seasons meant his massive potential was never fulfilled. Not once in his Liverpool career did his fitness problems allow him to string more than a dozen consecutive appearances together, so that the fans only saw a few tantalising glimpses of his exceptional talent.

The big-hearted waif

At 21, Walsh had every chance of developing into the worthiest of successors to the great Dalglish; at 25 he was limping his way out of the club, leaving behind little but frustrating thoughts of what might have been. Although he never had Kenny's physical strength, his skills could legitimately aspire to the class of the Glaswegian master. A busy, buzzing player who could bustle and fizz his way around the pitch for the full hour and a half, his energy and athleticism alone would have made him a handful for any defender, but he was also blessed with fantastic acceleration and a selection of cheeky tricks.

With his twisting, shimmying dribbles, Paul was among the slipperiest of Division One customers. He possessed the ability to control, turn and set off on the attack in seemingly the same movement and was devastating when running at the heart of a defence with the ball at his feet. Dalglish was – wrongly as it happened – perceived to be heading for his twilight years as a Red, and so impressive were his replacement's credentials that fans and pundits alike were convinced that a Walsh Rush strikeforce could prove even more potent than the Welshman's previous rapport with the great Scot. However, Paul's big break actually came at the expense of Rush, who found

Paul Walsh combined electric pace with impish skills and was earmarked as a natural successor to Kenny Dalglish. Sadly, a string of serious injuries ensured that his massive potential was never fulfilled.

Walsh bursts clear of the Ipswich Town defence during his first season at Anfield. Despite being denied a long run in the team he still scored at a respectable rate of better than a goal every three games.

himself sidelined by a cartilage problem at the start of the 1984-85 campaign. Lining up alongside Dalglish, the new man netted within an astonishing 15 seconds of his home debut against West Ham United, but 11 games later he picked up his first Anfield injury, which – coupled with the return of Rush – restricted him to just another dozen starts across the remaining seven months of the season.

Facing up to physical trials

That tale was to become a depressingly familiar one throughout the rest of his Liverpool days, blighted as they were by surgery to his ankle, knee and stomach and a broken wrist all inside a nightmare three years. A contributing factor to that unenviable record was undoubtedly the slightness of his 5ft 7in frame, which was simply not built to withstand the battering he would inevitably take as the focal point of the most feared attack in Europe. Although he made up in heart for almost everything he lacked in physical strength, Walsh could be muscled off the ball and often tended to drift out of the game under such punishment. That was as frustrating for the player as it was for the fans and he did remarkably well to retain his temper under often extreme provocation, snapping only once, in a League Cup semi-final at Southampton, when he floored Kevin Bond with a perfect right hook. The little striker left the field of play on a stretcher more often than he did in the face of a red card, and the saddest departure was the one he made on 9 February 1986, with an injury that both abruptly ended his most impressive run of form and sent his Anfield career into what proved to be terminal decline. Walsh took a particularly fierce buffeting from a mean Manchester United defence that day and although Liverpool triumphed through a single goal scored in the 40th minute, Paul had by that time been carried from the fray with badly damaged ankle ligaments.

In the 16 games before his injury, the agile little striker had scored 11 goals and was setting matches alight by delivering the sustained promise he had shown only in bursts the previous year. So outstanding had he been in that spell – which included a virtuoso two-goal display in a 3-2 win at Watford – that even though he played only twice more that season and missed out on the Double-winning FA Cup final, the Professional Footballers' Association still saw fit to include him in their First Division all-star XI.

Unfulfilled promise

Memories of the season in which that tribute was paid haunted Paul with dreams of its myriad unfulfilled possibilities, for he never quite recaptured the same form ever again. He scored a fine hat-trick in his orchestration of a 6-2 demolition of Norwich the following season but persistent injury problems left him having to prove himself all over again every time he made it out of the treatment room. The writing was on the wall for him in 1987, when manager Kenny Dalglish responded to the departure of Ian Rush to Juventus by buying John Aldridge, John Barnes and Peter Beardsley. Within six months Paul had moved on to Spurs for £500,000, although he took with him as many happy memories as regrets.

For the fans too, there were many warming recollections; particularly of spectacular hat-tricks against West Bromwich Albion and Brighton – the second haul including two goals in as many minutes – and a rampaging European Cup show against Austria Vienna in which he scored twice before squandering his treble chance from the penalty spot. Like that match, Paul Walsh's entire Liverpool career was something of a hit-and-miss affair. Few of the misses were his fault, and the hits when they came really were ones to remember. His story remains a tale of what might have been, but what there was revealed more than enough to mark him out as one of the rarer talents the club has seen.

Career History

Born: Plumstead, 1 October 1962
Signed: May 1984, from Luton Town
Full debut: Norwich City 3 Liverpool 3,
Division One, 25 August 1984
Games: 103 (18 as sub)
Goals: 35

International Caps

Five England caps, one goal

Honours

League Championship 1985-86

Other Clubs

Charlton Athletic, Luton Town, Tottenham Hotspur, Portsmouth, Manchester City, Portsmouth

Ronnie Whelan

Ronnie Whelan's Liverpool career was both a sprint for success and a marathon of endurance. While he exploded out of his Anfield blocks in the most sensational style to star in the winning of four major trophies in his first two senior seasons, the solid reliability that became his byword in later years was just as significant, if less spectacular, an influence on at least as many of Liverpool's subsequent successes. The skilful Irishman scored on his debut by racing 40 yards to slip Sammy Lee's through pass beneath the advancing Stoke goalkeeper in April 1981, and the following season he netted twice in the League Cup final, earned himself a first Championship medal and was named Young Player of the Year by the Professional Footballers' Association. Another winning Wembley goal in 1983 marked him out as a young man for the big occasion, a reputation he confirmed with several more important goals during the remainder of the first half of that decade.

As the years went by, however, the changes in personnel that began with the departure of Graeme Souness in 1984 gradually made Whelan one of the more experienced members of the side and he responded to the extra responsibility he was required to shoulder by maturing into a far more complete, and especially a more defensively adept, type of player. That perhaps blunted his attacking edge, for his goalscoring returns in the late 1980s and early 1990s were meagre shadows of the totals he notched up as a youngster, but without the grittier and less glamorous qualities he added to his game in those years he would not have been such an indispensable cog in the Anfield machinery.

Storing talent in reserve

To say that Ronnie encountered success beyond his wildest dreams would be by no means any sort of understatement, for when he crossed the Irish Sea as an uncertain teenager in 1979 his ambition did not stretch further than managing a couple of seasons in the reserves. In fact, it was only the efforts of the youngster's father, ex-international Ron senior, that actually got him to Anfield in the first place and then prevented him from walking out during an initial six months of extreme homesickness. Ronnie was not convinced that he had any real chance of making the grade at Liverpool

Ronnie Whelan helps Graeme Souness parade the League Cup after the 1982 defeat of Tottenham. The 20 year old scored twice in that game and hit another winner against Manchester United in the following season's final.

and his father only persuaded him to sign on the grounds that a footballing education at the finest academy in Europe might help him pick up another club a couple of years down the line. Within 18 months, that plan had gone out of the window as the versatile Dubliner made his debuts for both club and country within weeks of each other.

Whelan could in fact have been making his rapid progress with Manchester United in an irony that could not have gone unnoticed at Old Trafford as he curled a delicious 20-yarder past Gary Bailey to seal Liverpool's 1983 Milk Cup final victory over their arch rivals. As a schoolboy, Ronnie had trained with United during his holidays and actually

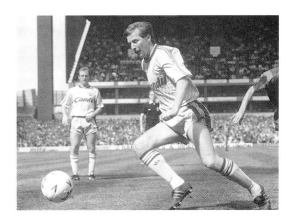

Whelan matured from the goalscoring midfielder of his youth to a ball-winning midfield general in his later years at Anfield. His contribution in that role was often unsung but never undervalued.

declined an offer to join them in order to stay in education. But by the time Liverpool came calling, he had left school and was actively looking for a move to England.

The move he eventually decided to make could not have been a better one, as the 12 major honours that grace his trophy cabinet readily attest. His early nerves persisted – he could not sleep the night before the 1982 League Cup final and began suffering butterflies in his stomach from the moment the twin towers came in sight – but from his composed performances on the pitch no one could ever have guessed it.

Golden goals

His first goal in that 3-1 win over Spurs coolly levelled the match with just three minutes remaining while his second, to give Liverpool the lead in extra-time, was despatched even more calmly as he even took time to steady himself before finishing off the Dalglish cross that had been deflected to him just inside the box. Such exquisite timing was on display again in the 1984 European Cup quarter-final against Benfica, when the single-goal lead the Reds took to Lisbon had them preparing for a 90-minute siege of Alamo proportions. Within three minutes Whelan's header – admittedly helped by bizarre goalkeeping from Bento – altered the entire complexion of the tie and the match finished 4-1 in the Anfield side's favour, with Whelan giving a neat symmetry to the scoresheet by adding its final entry with just three minutes to play.

Two-footed and blessed with such a sharp eye that he was actually more effective when volleying a pass at pace than when striking a dead ball, Ronnie found the net from midfield a useful 55 times in his first five full seasons. But by the last of those campaigns, 1985-86, he was beginning to establish himself as more of a creator than a finisher in that position, and emphasised the fact by providing the accurate crossfield pass from which Ian Rush wrapped up that season's FA Cup final against Everton.

Whelan was never the quickest of players and was always more likely to feed his forwards on early balls played perceptively through the inside-left channel rather than serve up a diet of crosses hit at speed from the bye-line. Those were the sort of balls that Rush thrived on, and

'Dusty' – the nickname he was landed with by the way his Dublin accent pronounced the word 'just' – had both the vision and the skill to pick him out on a regular basis. Ronnie's distribution came more to the fore after the departure of playmaker Souness. In 1987 he took over the central role that had once belonged to the player he had most admired, so that John Barnes could slot in on the left. Although never the biggest of players, the lad from the Home Farm amateur club packed plenty of power into his slim frame and he quickly began to develop into a solid and determined tackler in his new position.

The fresh responsibilities he had to attend to, coupled with the presence of so many great creative talents around him, meant that less was seen of his attacking play in the later years of his career and many observers in the Anfield stands began to suggest that his influence was starting to wane. In that respect he was underrated, for his unselfish grafting and creation of space for others through his intelligent running off the ball never gave him the high profile his dazzling shooting and passing had previously earned.

The team's unsung anchor man was thought of highly enough by his team-mates and manager to be handed the captaincy when Alan Hansen was struck down by injury in the 1988-89 campaign. That gave Whelan his proudest moment in the red jersey and he had extra cause to celebrate when holding aloft the FA Cup at Wembley that year: fitness problems of his own had deprived him of an appearance in the previous season's showpiece. The 1989-90 Championship was to prove his swansong, however, although another four years passed before he finally threw in the towel at Anfield and moved to Southend United, where he soon became player-manager. He saved Liverpool's bacon with a late equaliser in the 1992 FA Cup semi-final against Portsmouth, but missed the final itself through one of the injuries that dogged his last years with the Reds. Whelan's determination had earlier helped him overcome a career-threatening pelvic problem, but this time advancing age made his battle for fitness doubly difficult, and when he did play he often appeared overweight and increasingly off the pace.

Graeme Souness transfer-listed him in September 1993 and when he failed in the following summer to reach agreement with the new management over the length of contract that they were prepared to offer, he reluctantly decided that it was time to take his leave of the club. After a decade and a half of sterling service, Ronnie Whelan had stayed for 13 years longer than he had originally anticipated. His outstanding dedication and skill ensured that even after all those years he was never in any danger of outstaying his welcome.

Career History

Born: Dublin, 25 September 1961

Signed: October 1979

Full debut: Liverpool 3 Stoke City 0, Division One, 3 April 1981

Games: 477 (17 as sub)

Goals: 72

International Caps

53 Republic of Ireland caps, three goals

Honours

European Cup 1983-84; League Championship 1981-82, 1982-83, 1983-84, 1985-86, 1987-88, 1989-90; FA Cup 1985-86, 1988-89; League Cup 1981-82, 1982-83, 1983-84

Other Club

Southend United

Mark Wright

The fee quoted on the transfer forms that made Mark Wright a Liverpool player in the summer of 1991 is a cool two million, two hundred thousand pounds; by contrast, the remarkable comeback that has rebuilt his Anfield career cost just £300 and a bottle of Jack Daniels. The tall defender crowned his first season as a Red by captaining his side to victory in the FA Cup final, only to see the fortunes of himself, his manager and the entire club go into immediate freefall. Roy Evans' appointment as manager halted the collective rot, but Wright's personal decline continued and reached its nadir in the summer of 1994, when he and full-back Julian Dicks were thrown off the pre-season tour for perceived attitude problems.

Wright had been fighting a losing battle against what was apparently a serious achilles tendon injury for the better part of the previous six months and with that bust-up leaving him apparently unwanted as well as unfit, his days at Anfield appeared to be numbered. However, although Dicks was quickly shipped out to West Ham, Mark bravely elected to stay with the Reds and struggle on to overcome his problems of first fitness and then selection.

A bottle of cheer

By December, the wisdom of that decision appeared increasingly questionable as he had made frustratingly little progress on either front, and the signing of John Scales and Phil Babb looked like the broadest of hints to begin packing his bags. But things started to change from the moment he turned in desperation to the blind physiotherapist who it turned out would save his career for the price of the aforementioned modest cash sum and bottle of bourbon. Norman Collins, whose degeneration of the optic nerve has restricted his sight to the point that he is registered blind, is well known for his work with sportsmen and managed to put Wright on the road to recovery within a week. The injury had been suffered in a match against Arsenal in March 1994 and although the player was feeling it in his achilles – an area that had caused him trouble in the past – the pain was actually being transmitted from a knot of scar tissue higher up the leg. With the problem thus identified, hard work at Melwood quickly had Wright training at full throttle for the first time in almost a year and his own determination then carried him back to the fringes of the first-team. The Reds paid Mr Collins £300 for his efforts and the delighted player presented him with the Jack Daniels as a thank-you gift.

A trademark Mark Wright intervention dispossesses the Sunderland winger Peter Davenport during the 1992 FA Cup final. The Reds' 2-0 victory in that game crowned the England international's first season at Anfield, during which he had captained the side.

Wright knew he had much to be grateful for, as the physiotherapy had readied him for one last chance, at the age of 31, to resurrect his Liverpool career. But when that final opportunity eventually knocked in the form of an injury to Scales in March 1995, the success with which he seized the moment was achieved purely under his own steam. His display against Manchester United that day was near flawless and another close-season injury to Scales saw him handed a starting place in the side that began the 1995-96 campaign. Mark continued where he left off, defending with such skill and composure that Scales, Babb and Neil Ruddock were forced to scrap among themselves for the remaining two places in the Reds' three-man back line. Wright quickly established himself as an automatic choice who could play either on the right or in the middle of the trio, and in 41 matches that term was only just edged out of the *Liverpool Echo*'s player of the year award by Steve McManaman. Rarely ever flustered, the tall centre-half remained as dominant as ever in the air but now added composure and intelligence to his work on the ground, reading the play superbly to cover for his colleagues and push attackers into areas from where they could produce little danger and in which he could happily dispossess them with one of his trademark sliding tackles.

He also impressed in bringing the ball out of defence, moving forward with assurance to set attacks in motion, and weighed in with an occasional goal of his own, including a fierce curling drive at Queens Park Rangers in February 1996 and the late header that gave Liverpool a brief glimpse of hope in the European Cup Winners' Cup semi-final defeat by Paris Saint Germain 14 months later.

However, Mark Wright's success in a three-man central defensive arrangement should really have come as little surprise, for it was in a similar system operated by England during the 1990 World Cup that he first came to real prominence. The class he showed in playing his way into the tournament's all star XI prompted Graeme Souness to bring him to Anfield from Derby County the following summer. Although his first season ended in FA Cup success, the new boy never looked quite the player he had in Italia '90 when employed in the middle of a conventional back four. His heading and recovery tackling impressed but he lacked a yard in pace and could be caught on the turn, as Southampton's Matt Le Tissier cruelly demonstrated at Anfield in October 1993.

A crisis of confidence

During the final 18 months of Souness' reign, Wright's game suffered the same loss of confidence that afflicted the Liverpool team as a whole and in his case the problem was compounded by the burden of captaining what was an increasingly unhappy ship. The sturdy centre-half had always been prone to occasional lapses in concentration and the task of having to take responsibility for his team-mates did not help him to keep his mind on his own defensive duties. Injury and argument soon relieved him of first the captaincy and then his place in the side, and when he did make his comeback it benefited both player and team that he did so in a three-man rearguard.

Wright returned to show arguably the best form of his career during 1995-96 and 1996-97 and confirmation of that fact came when England coach Terry Venables recalled him to the national side he had last represented four years earlier. Again operating in a three-man back line, he performed with all the class of a player who had previously been rated among the finest defenders in the world and only injury deprived him of a place in England's Euro '96 squad.

Venables' successor Glenn Hoddle declined to follow his selectoral lead the following term but the fact that his name remained in the international frame as he headed for his 34th birthday was proof enough that reports of Mark Wright's footballing demise had once again been greatly exaggerated.

Career History

Born: Dorchester, 1 August 1963
Signed: July 1991, from Derby County
Full debut: Liverpool 2 Oldham Athletic 1,
Division One, 17 August 1991
Games: 205 (six as sub)
Goals: eight

International Caps

45 England caps, one goal

Honours

FA Cup 1991-92

Other Clubs

Oxford United, Southampton, Derby County

Ron Yeats

When Ron Yeats stepped off the train at Lime Street in July 1961 none of the waiting crowd of autograph hunters and well-wishers needed to ask which of the passengers was Liverpool's new centre-half. The Reds had been surprisingly secretive about his transfer from Dundee United, keeping silent about the size of the fee and suggesting that he would be flying into the city after putting pen to paper in Scotland. But men of Yeats' stature are difficult to hide and even though the fans at the station were thus far unfamiliar with his work, it did not take them long to pick him out on the platform.

A massive presence

At 6ft 2in and 14st 5lb, Shankly was for once not exaggerating when he invited the press to take a walk round his new signing. Yeats was a giant of a man. And in all senses, as Anfield was soon to discover. It wasn't his enormous frame and massive physical presence that earned him the club captaincy within five months of his arrival; he was a genuinely great leader of men. However, it was the hard outer shell, rather than the inner man it protected, which made Ron Yeats' name and by which he is first remembered; understandably so as he did cut the most imposing of figures.

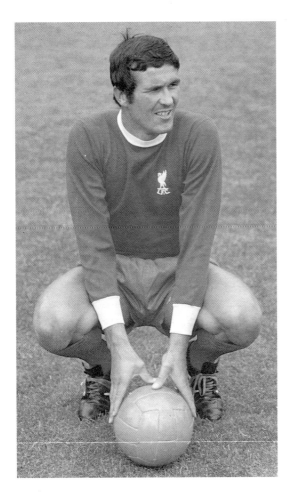

It is no coincidence that almost all the metaphors ever used to characterise him focus solely on his appearance and spring from the language of bricks, mortar and the toughest of masonry. He was his manager's 'Colossus' and 'the cornerstone of the building up of this club', to his players he was a simpler 'big man'. He was variously described as the foundation of Liverpool's success in the 1960s, a tower of strength in the air and the rock on which many an opposition attack would founder. His background did little to divert his admirers from such imagery, hailing as he did from the granite city of Aberdeen, where he had been apprenticed into the family trade of slaughterman before turning to football professionally.

Ron Yeats was the giant defender immortalised by Bill Shankly's famous offer to show reporters round him. But the former slaughterman was as big in personality as physique and became one of Liverpool's finest leaders.

The impact Anfield made on the newly arrived Yeats was no smaller than the impact he would make on it. The £30,000 Liverpool paid to acquire his services at the second

Yeats led by example on the field of play breaking up attacks with his solid tackling and being so commanding in the air that goalkeeper Tommy Lawrence left him to deal with almost all crosses that entered the box.

attempt came hot on the heels of the club record £37,500 they had just shelled out for Ian St John. Both players were instant hits and were instrumental in helping the Reds to the Second Division Championship at the end of their first season together. But the comparatively big money the Reds spent on their even bigger centre-half did not buy them a complete player. Ron confesses that it was only after arriving at Anfield that he began to appreciate the game's tactical nuances, and training proved something of a culture shock as well. Shankly may have eschewed the traditional routine of endless shuttle runs and laps of the ground, but his preferred regime of five-a-sides and even exercises based on boxing work-outs was no less exhausting, and Yeats – who was by no means unfit – was still suffering almost a month after he arrived. Coming on top of the Melwood training load, his debut on 19 August 1961 left him so exhausted that he spent the entire return coach journey from Bristol Rovers stretched out across the back seats sleeping like a baby.

A long-lasting investment

But that afternoon he had already demonstrated that the board's money had been well spent and as the backbone of that Liverpool side he quickly became a cult hero on the Kop. More than any other player, he symbolised the power, efficiency and professionalism that was the driving force behind the new Liverpool FC, missing only 20 games in his first six years at the club. He and St John were the men credited as the catalysts for the Reds' successful promotion push and the fans showed their appreciation after the match that clinched the Division Two title, swarming on to the pitch during the players' attempted lap of honour and sweeping the two Scots away with such exuberance that they had to be rescued by the police.

The experience surprised even Yeats, but his playing attributes and full-blooded commitment had won him that sort of affection in double-quick time. As might be expected from a man of his size, he took more than a stride to get into top gear. When he got going, though, he was seldom left struggling for speed. A combination of positional awareness and exceptional powers of recovery ensured that such questions were rarely posed in the first place. His distribution was the more effective for never being over-ambitious and displayed a healthy awareness of his own limitations, but it was in his traditional defensive duties that he really excelled.

The quiet giant

Ron always made the most of his height and power in the air and the tackles with which he swept away danger from his favoured left-hand side had a ferocious finality about them. Yeats was never a dirty player but he was a genuine hard man who commanded the respect of friend and foe. Peter Thompson once tired of trying to dribble round the big man in training and reasoned that the quickest way past him was to push the ball through his legs and collect it on the other side. Before he could make off towards goal he found his progress halted by a large hand round his throat. 'Don't do that again,' growled big Ron. Thompson didn't.

His feeling for the team could only rub off on those around him and marked him out as a potential captain early on. Yeats always insisted that the leader of Liverpool had merely to toss a coin before kick-off, and maintained that he only ever had to shout at a colleague once, and that was over a misunderstanding for which he later apologised. That may be true, but only because he had the complete trust and respect of his peers. It was he rather than Shankly to whom younger players would turn with their problems, and even the older hands were kept in line by the fear of having to explain themselves to the big man.

He was the first Liverpool captain to hold aloft the FA Cup, a moment that he later described as the proudest of his life. His Anfield career ended in 1971 after growing back trouble eventually cost him his place and signalled a move to Tranmere Rovers as player-manager. He returned to Liverpool during the mid-1980s to become Chief Scout. Should he ever unearth another defender with the same strength of body and mind as Ron Yeats, it would prove to be a rare find indeed.

Career History

Born: Aberdeen, 15 November 1937
Signed: July 1961, from Dundee United
Full debut: Bristol Rovers 0 Liverpool 2, Division Two, 19 August 1961
Games: 451 (one as sub)
Goals: 15

International Caps

Two Scotland caps

Honours

League Championship 1963-64, 1965-66; FA Cup 1964-65

Other Clubs

Dundee United, Tranmere Rovers